A Pictorial History of Middletown

The publication of this book was made possible by these sponsors

———————————

Bernie Fields Jewelers

———————————

Middlesex Mutual Assurance Company

———————————

The Prudential-Connecticut Realty, Middletown Office

———————————

Vision Corner

———————————

Wesleyan University

———————————

A special grant was provided by

Northeast Utilities

———————————

❏

The records of our past, both printed and constructed, help us discern our place in the present. The sponsors are proud to have a part in preserving the history and architecture of Middletown through presentation of this pictorial account of the city's development. We hope this book will encourage interest in and appreciation of Middletown's residential and commercial neighborhoods. The book itself becomes a record—for our children, grandchildren and all who come after us—a record of our first three hundred years.

This panorama of Middletown and the river's bend was published by Lucius R. Hazen in 1896. Hazen, a local printer and advertiser, published Views of Middletown, *a booklet of five-by-seven photographs, including this one, representing Middletown's neighborhoods and institutions. During the next twenty-five years, several local businesses and banks also provided souvenir booklets of Middletown views, yet none compared in composition and print quality with Hazen's photographs.*
Courtesy Everett Wright

THE
DONNING COMPANY
PUBLISHERS
NORFOLK / VIRGINIA BEACH

A Pictorial History of Middletown

by
Elizabeth A. Warner
for
The Greater Middletown Preservation Trust

This book is warmly dedicated to J. Russell "Doc" Ward. Doc has always shared his enthusiasm for and has inspired others with his love of Middletown history.

Copyright © 1990 by the Greater Middletown Preservation
    Trust
All rights reserved, including the right to reproduce this work
in any form whatsoever without permission in writing from
the publisher, except for brief passages in connection with a
review. For information, write:
    The Donning Company/Publishers
    5659 Virginia Beach Boulevard
    Norfolk, Virginia 23502

Edited by Richard A. Horwege
Designed by L. J. Wiley

Library of Congress Cataloging in Publication Data:

Warner, Elizabeth A. (Elizabeth Ann), 1956-
    A pictorial history of Middletown / by Elizabeth A. Warner.
        p. cm.
    Includes bibliographical references and index.
    ISBN 0-89865-801-2
    1. Middletown (Conn.)—History—Pictorial works. 2.
Middletown (Conn.)—Description—Views. I. Title.
F104.M6W37   1990   90-3335
974.6'6—dc20   CIP

Printed in the United States of America

Contents

... Industrial School for Girls ... in 1892, i... ow Long Lane ... coeducational correctional facility administered by the state of Connecticut. The girls at Connecticut Industrial School for Girls lived in family-type cottages, and they were given the "special physical, mental, moral, social and industrial training necessary to fit them for life". (1896 Middletown Tribune Souvenir Edition).
From Parish, Scenes of Middlesex County, courtesy Greater Middletown Preservation Trust

Foreword

by Annie Dillard

◻

In 1790 it was the biggest city in Connecticut. Yankee settlers built ships here to carry local lumber and cattle to the West Indies. There were salmon and shad fisheries, textile mills, and lots of cattle and sheep. Across the river they quarried brownstone, barged it downriver, and built Manhattan with it. All that ended; people left. Then Middletown became a manufacturing center—the world's leader, in fact, in the production of elastic webbing. Which, in the form of suspenders, kept your pants up. Factories made sleigh bells, locks, tinware, noiseless typewriters, and swords. That ended, too, as patterns of industry changed. Today townspeople work for Pratt and Whitney, making jet engine parts, or Aetna Life & Casualty, Xerox, or Wesleyan University.

Now Middletown is a Sicilian town, and an Irish town, a Polish town, an Eastern European Jewish town, a Western European town, a Greek town, an Afro-American (via Barbados) town, an English town.

The Memorial Day parade looks like a multicolored parade of how this country might work. The kids are wearing Scout uniforms, Little League uniforms, majorette costumes, clown suits; their fathers march with the Veterans of Foreign Wars. Here are tall black men and women walking with stocky Italian men and women; they are all wearing buckskin leggings and carrying long rifles. Here are Polish kids in kilts playing bagpipes, or, more commonly, Polish kids marching with Polish parents under Polish banners, in line behind hospital volunteers, random horsemen, 4-H'ers, or a Greek men's club, a fife-and-drum corps, a high-stepping high school band. It all makes an exuberant music—the big drums knocking at your rib cage—and it all makes an exhilarating spectacle, for the mind as well as the eyes, suggestive and bright, as if all the colorful books in a big bookstore were tooting and twirling down Main Street.

It works . . . .

From "Why I Live Where I Live," Esquire, *March 1984.*
Copyright © by The Hearst Corporation. Used with permission.

Hubbard Brothers, dealers in lumber and building supplies, was located at the foot of Williams Street, close to the wharves and railroad lines. After the company closed in 1878, the former president, Gaston T. Hubbard, invested his capital in Rogers and Hubbard, which ground bone and ivory for fertilizer in the former factory of the Wilcox Lock Company on Pamaecha Creek.
Courtesy J. Russell "Doc" Ward

Preface

❏

Since its inception in 1972, one of the primary objectives of the Greater Middletown Preservation Trust has been to foster greater public awareness of history and architecture. While this book is a departure from our earlier History and Architecture series, it is very much an outgrowth of that effort. With *A Pictorial History of Middletown* we present the personal side of Middletown's history hoping that our appreciation of that legacy will be broadened by the opportunity to see Middletown from a different perspective.

We would like to thank our sponsors, Bernie Fields Jewelers, Middlesex Mutual Assurance Company, the Middletown Office of The Prudential-Connecticut Realty, Vision Corner, and Wesleyan University, whose commitments to Middletown made this book possible. We would also like to acknowledge a special grant from Northeast Utilities which provided much needed support early in the project.

I would like to personally thank author Liz Warner and photographer Matt Polansky for their energy and professional skills, and Debra Quesnel of the Donning Company whose enthusiasm encouraged us to undertake the project nearly two years ago. Thanks also to Trust board members and other friends for their help along the way, particularly to JoAn Chace, C. Lee Heald, Peter Frenzel and Susan McNamara.

Ann C. Street
Executive Director

Main Street had always been the site of Middletown's public buildings, but it remained residential in character until the Civil War. After that time, wood frame houses were gradually replaced with brick or stone commercial buildings, providing Main Street with the general appearance we know today. This photograph, taken from the second story of the Brewer building at the northeast corner of Main and Court streets in 1887, shows (from left to right) the Universalist Church at the corner of College Street, Nehemiah Hubbard, Jr.'s residence (with columns), the Court House, the Middletown National Bank (set back), the Bank Block, and the Custom House. All the buildings, except the Universalist Church, have been torn down. The deconsecrated church now serves as offices for McCutcheon and Burr, Inc., and is part of Plaza Middlesex. The last building to be torn down in this neighborhood was Nehemiah Hubbard, Jr.'s house—razed in 1986 to make way for the addition to Farmers and Mechanics Savings Bank.
Courtesy Robert Chamberlain

Acknowledgments

❑

Middletown is blessed with many friends of history - people who have protected the remnants of its past and were willing to share them with me for this publication. More than one hundred individuals and institutions responded to the *Middletown Press* articles about the book project and offered assistance through the use of historic photographs or historical information. Truly, the most treasured moments of this project have been those afternoons sitting with local families and reminiscing about times gone by. Although I was not around in the 1920s, 1930s, or 1940s, through the warmth with which they told their stories, their life experiences have become part of mine. For this I thank all those who invited me in and honored me with their recollections.

I wish to thank Robert Adams, Wesleyan University Librarian, for allowing me to use the university's extensive Middletown collection in Special Collections and Archives. Elizabeth Swain, Special Collections Librarian and University Archivist, and her assistant Diana Perron, helped me weed through the enormous amount of material and offered valuable suggestions. Brenda Milkofsky and her staff from the Connecticut River Museum at the Steamboat Dock in Essex were most helpful by allowing me use of materials from their collections and exhibits.

The *Middletown Press*, through the cooperation of Russell "Derry" D'Oench, made me feel at home in their archives and lent many fine photographs for the book. Special thanks to Marcella

Marks and Cathy Cienava for helping me through many panicky moments. I extend thanks to Bill Cornelius of Middlesex Mutual Assurance Company for providing me with material while he and his staff were in the midst of moving into their new offices. I am grateful to Bernie Fields for always being able to work wonders.

Sincere thanks go to J. Russell "Doc" Ward for allowing me access to his personal collection, which provided forty-five photographs for the book and two of the most enjoyable days of my life as I browsed through it. Colonel Chester B. McCoid made his collection of memorabilia, which includes business trade cards, postcards, railroad photographs, and Westfield and general town views, available to me. He shared his extensive knowledge of Middletown's development and connected me to other people who had additional photographs. I am grateful to Everett Wright who shared his fine collection of Middletown postcards and his Lucian R. Hazen views of 1896. Bill Batty, who worked for Wilcox, Crittenden and Company for over forty years, allowed me use of his photographic collection and gave me hours of pleasurable listening. I wish to extend my appreciation to Frank and Mildred Roberts, Bill Fortin, Judi Elder, Helen Raffuse, Betty Bacon, Muriel Schulman, Estelle Goodman, and Ted and Anne Nowakowski for photographs and enjoyable afternoons.

The staff of the Russell Library's information department provided not only assistance, but cheerful encouragement throughout the project.

Deborah Ritter, Head of the Information Department, and her staff, Helen Pribram, Vickie Doddman, Phyllis Nathanson, Marcie Kenney, and George Galvin provided me with answers to my endless questions. When I was stuck at the computer, they were only a phone call away.

I appreciate the skill and efficiency with which Matt Polansky reproduced hundreds of photographs, often in less than convenient circumstances. I will forever be indebted to Susan McNamara, who donated endless hours to editing my manuscript. There were times when she had to drag from me the information and stories that she knew were inside. Anything that sparks of life in this book is due to her patience and determination.

One need only look in one's back yard for the answers to most of life's questions. My parents, Clint and Barbara (Molander) Warner, certainly proved this to be true. They patiently searched their childhood memories for Middletown people and places and reconstructed the world in which they grew. They fielded my calls, which came at all hours of the day and night, and gave me support and encouragement.

The most cooperative and patient bystander was my 2½-year-old daughter, Adriana Najera, who took it in her stride when I was working at the computer and unavailable for play. Special thanks to my husband Alberto Najera for supporting my efforts while the book consumed our lives.

Liz Warner

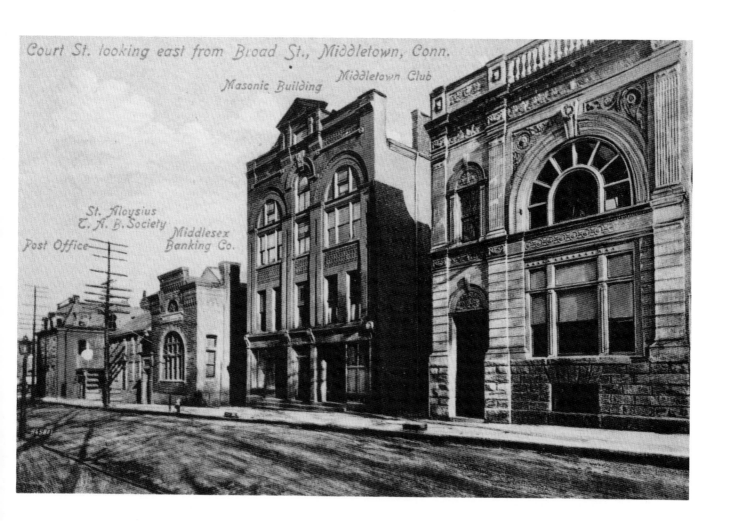

Court St. looking east from Broad St., Middletown, Conn.

Masonic Building   Middletown Club

St. Aloysius
T. A. B. Society
Post Office   Middlesex
Banking Co.

This lithograph by Fr. Meyer, published in 1856, shows the sheltered harbor and the great bend in the Connecticut River at Middletown. The view was drawn from *Fort Hill, where the Connecticut Valley Hospital was later built.*
Courtesy Ann Moskal Salonia

1

The Early Years
1650 to 1820
❑

The Land and Its People

The geographical features of Middletown, including the great bend in the Connecticut River, were created over thousands of years during the Ice Age. Increasingly, geologists are able to develop hypotheses to explain the forces of nature that formed the environment as we know it. A fault line, linear in depth, runs north-northwest, and south-southeast, from Old Saybrook to Middletown. Above the surface, this fault line is evidenced by the rectilinear path of the river from Middletown, as compared to its meandering path above Middletown, particularly in the Springfield, Massachusetts region. The fault valley south of Middletown is characterized by the steep pitch of rocks along the river's edge and the river's relatively straight course to Long Island Sound. The fault caused the region near Middletown to be a zone of weakness during the last glacial period, almost twenty thousand years ago. Prior to that time, the river's path ran straight at Glastonbury, east of the present town of Portland. At East Hampton it connected with the present stretch of the river to Old Saybrook. When the glaciers in New England began to melt, meltwater formed lakes and rivers in the larger valleys. Drifts of stone, sand, and clay washed into the valley near Middletown and dammed the water's flow at its narrowest point, in the area known as the Straits or Narrows. A long, narrow lake, called Lake Hitchcock by geologists, filled the Connecticut River Valley from Lyme,

The Narrows of the Connecticut River between the Maromas section of Middletown and East Hampton also marks a fault line running north-northwest by south-southeast and separating two distinct geological regions. The area south-southeast of the Straits sits on a granite bedrock. In this photograph, granite outcroppings are visible at the upper reservoir on Bear Hill Road in Maromas.
Courtesy Rick Mazzotta, Dark Eyes Images

New Hampshire, to Middletown. It was during this period that the great bend at Middletown was formed from water filling a deep valley. Geologists believe about ten thousand years ago the dam gradually began to erode, eventually breaking through with catastrophic force. The lake's waters, driven southward toward the Narrows, changed the course of the river, diverting it into the existing valley at Middletown. As the waters of the lake receded, clay was deposited, providing rich alluvial soil in the river valley. □

Native Americans

Native Americans in the woodland areas of the Northeast comprised two basic language groups, Iroquoian and Algonquian. The Iroquois lived in upstate New York, while the Algonquians (also spelled *Algonkian* or *Algonkin*) made their way eastward into New England and Canada. The Algonquian tribes throughout the Northeast developed distinct dialects and lifestyles.

When the first Puritan settlers arrived in 1650 at what later became known as Middletown, the region was inhabited by the Wangunk tribe of Algonquian-speaking natives. The Wangunks called the area *Massabesec* or *Massabesett*, translated as "at a great river or brook." *Massa*, meaning "great," was often corrupted to "matta" by the English tongue. The "ec" ending referred to tidal rivers, such as the Connecticut. The settlers spelled this topographical description in various ways: first as *Mattabesicke*, then in 1646 as *Matabezeke*, and in 1657 as *Mattapeaset*.

The Algonquians were a spiritual people, closely bound to their clan and to nature. The clan identified itself with an animal symbol, or totem, as its spiritual guardian and supernatural ancestor. Life was directed by Manitou, or the Great Spirit,

who was found in all living things and in the forces of nature. Legends answered the questions of life, and explained good and evil. Rituals commemorated life's important events, such as planting, harvesting, war, and coming of age.

The Wangunk skillfully used local resources. They shaped stones and animal bones into tools versatile enough to carve birch or elm bark canoes in just a few days. The canoe was used by the Wangunk for fishing, trading, and war. With stone tools they honed razor-sharp arrowheads that were attached to wooden spears and used as weapons to kill game or fight battles. Arrowheads are still found in local fields and yards.

The Wangunk lived by hunting game, gathering fruits and nuts, and farming. White-tailed deer were killed for food and clothing. The hides were cured into soft leather, or buckskin, and used for everything from breechcloths to wigwam insulation. Uncured pelts were used for fur robes. Close to the river, where the spring freshet guaranteed fertile soil, beans, corn, and squash were planted beyond the cluster of wigwams. The permanent village at Middletown was probably less than one hundred people, each family occupying its own wigwam.

Life in Wangunk society changed little over many thousands of years. But in the late sixteenth century, there was a migration of Mohegan Indians from the upper Hudson River Valley into Connecticut. The Algonquians called them *Pequots*, meaning "destroyers of men." The Pequots established their villages in southeastern Connecticut, near the Thames River, and dominated the Algonquians throughout Connecticut. Wangunk villages sprouted palisades as protection from Pequot attack.

Native Americans were decimated by European diseases spread by explorers and traders. Plagues of smallpox and yellow fever in 1616 and

Middletown and the region north-northwest of the great bend rest on a porous and pliable stone, called brownstone because of its deep chocolate color. Brownstone, particularly from the Portland quarries, was an important building material in the nineteenth century in use throughout the United States. The sedimentary layers in brownstone are clearly visible in this late-nineteenth-century photograph of the Shaler and Hall Quarry in Portland.
Photograph, circa 1890, courtesy J. Russell "Doc" Ward

1633 had already wiped out large numbers of the woodland tribes, leaving only between six thousand and fifteen thousand Native Americans in Connecticut when the European settlers arrived. The Wangunk way of life ended. Sowheag, the great chief of the Wangunks, surrendered the tribe's lands in Wethersfield in 1634 and relocated to Mattabeset, though he remained hostile to the settlers. When a small group of the local Wangunks aided a Pequot war party in a raid on Wethersfield that killed nine adults and captured two children, Sowheag harbored the Pequots. He relinquished all the lands in Middletown between 1650 and 1672, except for three hundred acres east of the river, and a strip of land through Newfield to Indian Hill Cemetery. It is from this last Indian village that the cemetery takes its name.

During the early years of settlement, threat of Indian attack was a constant fear. Attacks came primarily from the Pequot Indians, who saw the newcomers as a threat to their dominance. In September of 1676, a native was brought before the town leaders for killing John Kirby of Upper Houses (now Cromwell) while he traveled the road to Wethersfield, for burning the house of Mr. Coale, as well as for numerous robberies. The town ruled that "if the Indians see cause to put him to death, they shall do it forthwith; if not, he shall be shot to death by some English." (Records of the General Court, 1676) In that same year, the last of the Indian Wars ended, and the threat of Indian attack gradually subsided. By 1689, the settlers claimed the last of Sowheag's territory. Many Native American survivors were sold into slavery in the West Indies; others retreated to small reservations.

While historical accounts lead one to believe that by 1750 all Native Americans had disappeared

from the Connecticut towns, several local residents recall family stories about small Indian enclaves in Middletown well into the nineteenth century. As a little girl in the 1850s, Jane Baldwin Roberts learned herbal remedies from Indians living on the hill overlooking Kelsey Street. A small tribe resided near Crystal Lake in the mid-century, on land owned by the Brock family. (Howard Baldwin, 1989) □

Mattabesett to Middletown

In 1614 Adrian Block was the first European to sail up the Connecticut River, aboard the Dutch ship *Onrust*. The Dutch built an outpost at Hartford in 1633, the same year a small group of Englishmen came from Plymouth Colony to Windsor. The Massachusetts Bay Colony sent settlers in 1634 to found Wethersfield, and a larger group in 1635 to Hartford. Saybrook was the site of an English fort beginning in 1635. Over the next thirty-five years the area between Windsor and Saybrook was settled mainly by families from these early villages.

A settlement, called Mattabeseck, was established in 1651. When the land was officially granted by the General Court ten years later, the settlement was renamed Middletown for its location midway between Hartford and Saybrook. Its boundaries incorporated the present towns of Middletown, Cromwell, Middlefield, Portland, East Hampton, and a small portion of Berlin. The proprietors' houses were clustered together near the meeting house in the North End (near St. John's Church). When a man bought a home lot in Mattabeseck, he became a proprietor with a share in the new township. Furthermore, each of the fifty-two proprietors received additional land in proportion to the amount he had paid for his home lot. When all the land on the western side of the river was divided in 1662, and again when the land on the east side was divided in 1671 and 1674, those of wealth, who had purchased larger and more desirable parcels for their homes, received larger and more fertile tracts of farmland.

Most of the original proprietors came from the Wethersfield and Hartford settlements, the sons of men and women who had traveled to Connecticut from the Massachusetts Bay Colony. Like their fathers, they were sustained by their Puritan faith, eager to create a holy community based on literal interpretations of the Bible. The Puritans came primarily from well-educated families in England, often turning away from secure wealth and social standing to try this experiment in the New World. Originally English Puritans had separated from the Church of England to purify it of its Roman Catholic elements, particularly the hierarchy of religious leadership. In America, settlers sharing this concern established the Congregational Church, in which all members of a congregation had a voice in the activities of the church. However, the right to be a church member was based on strict moral requirements and on one's financial success. Only those who could prove to a church body that they had the grace of God were admitted as members, and only those with church membership were allowed to vote in church and town affairs. Attendance in church was mandatory, and social conformity was expected. Each man was his "brother's keeper," ensuring that everyone lived according to expectations. The church meted out punishments for social infractions, such as not attending church or having a disrespectful child.

One of the first goals of the Middletown settlers was to construct a meeting house for religious services and town business. The building, erected at the northern end of Main Street in 1652, was a ten-by-twenty-foot rectangular wooden structure that served the community until 1680. A second church was built on the east side of Main Street, opposite what is today Liberty Street; about 1720 it was replaced by yet another church on High Street, near Church Street.

During the first one hundred years the families of Middletown cleared thousands of acres of farmland. The original proprietor families each held several hundred acres in reserve to divide and pass to their sons. By the early eighteenth century, settlers had spread out along the river, establishing villages at Upper Houses (now Cromwell), Maromas, and East Hampton, as well as inland at Westfield and Middlefield. In England, where land was scarce, family estates were passed from father to eldest son by the law of primogeniture. Because land in America was plentiful, the New England colonists discarded primogeniture for an inheritance system that provided the possibility of land for all sons and dowries for each daughter. However, by 1750 Middletown land had been divided and subdivided among the proprietors' descendants. At a time when at least forty-five acres were needed for a family to subsist (for hay, pasture, firewood, and crop rotation), the population began to overburden the available land. ☐

Riverport Era

In the mid-eighteenth century the sons of Middletown farmers who no longer could depend on inheriting enough land to be prosperous farmers began looking beyond the land for their livelihood. Those sons with capital and forethought invested in shipbuilding and trade, developing a new economic base for the community. Newcomers came to Middletown to invest in the new business opportunities. Middletown's population swelled, transforming it from a rural village to a major riverport. Local sea captains joined the Triangle Trade between the colonies, the West Indies, and England, exchanging rum and farm products in the West Indies for slaves, sugar, and molasses. West Indian cargo was carried to England, along with Connecticut's plentiful raw materials, such as lumber and lead, which were converted in English mills to manufactured goods such as nails, books, and furniture, then sold back to the colonies. Middletown farmers and merchants relied on this trading network throughout the eighteenth century.

River trade provided men with careers as sailors and sea captains. Laborers were needed at the docks, coopers supplied barrels and hogsheads, and artisans—sailmakers, ropemakers, blacksmiths, and shipwrights—were required for shipbuilding.

Ships were built at yards in Middletown, Portland, and Cromwell, although Middle Haddam was the most successful commercial shipbuilding village, with six yards operating until 1825. The yards built sloops and schooners for coastal trading, and larger brigs and full-rigged ships for trade between the Indies and Europe.

Middletown men, such as Richard Alsop and Elijah Hubbard, made fortunes in shipping and trade. When Alsop died during the American Revolution, the inventory of his estate was fifty-one pages long. At a time when fifty pounds could buy a house on a small parcel of land, the estate was valued at over thirty-five thousand pounds, plus "a large amount of money in Jamaica." (Field, 1853) Samuel Russell, one of Middletown's most prosperous merchants, established a merchant house in Canton, China, importing Turkish

In 1851, John W. DeForest included this engraving in his History of the Indians in Connecticut. The Mohawk hairdo often depicted in paintings of Connecticut Indians by Englishmen was a style worn primarily by the Iroquois Indians, a tribe to the west.
Courtesy Russell Library and William Kehoe

Unlike the pointed tepees associated with western Plains Indians, the Algonquian wigwam, or wetus, was a dome-shaped dwelling made of bent saplings with birch or elm bark, or reed mats stretched between the poles. Animal skins over the top provided insulation from winter's cold, and hides or grass covered the floor.
Courtesy American Indian Archaeological Institute, used with permission

This drawing, from the estate of Mildred Meader, is believed to be of Middletown's first meeting house. The log represents the site set aside for Riverview Cemetery, the town's first burial place.
Courtesy First Congregational Church

and Bengali opium and exporting fine teas and silks to Europe and the United States. With the great wealth he acquired between 1818 and 1831, Russell invested in the Russell Manufacturing Company and local railroad enterprises. But his mansion at High and Washington streets was his most lasting contribution to Middletown. After his 1827 marriage, Samuel Russell sent seventy-five hundred dollars from China with instructions to his friend, Samuel Dickinson Hubbard, to have a

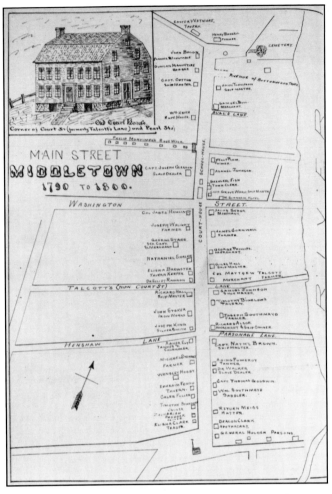

Main Street was laid out on the high ground parallel to the river. Homelots were set up on either side of the street and byways led to the river or westward to the interior of town. In 1836, Dr. Joseph Barratt drew this map of Main Street to represent its appearance at the time of the American Revolution. As the map indicates, people on Main Street lived and worked in the same structure. Main Street retained its residential character until the Civil War.
Courtesy J. Russell "Doc" Ward

"plain and neat" house built. Ignoring Russell's instructions, Hubbard and Mrs. Russell hired Ithiel Town, one of the nation's foremost architects, who constructed a home in the style of a Greek temple, and on a temple's monumental scale.

Hiring a formally-trained architect to design a residential structure was a new idea in 1827. Earlier American building designs were produced by builders drawing on traditional motifs or by the gentleman-scholar, an amateur versed in the visual elements of classical architecture, but sometimes lacking technical expertise. The building of the nation's Capitol and the need for new public buildings after the Revolution created a demand for architects to create original designs for the new nation. Ithiel Town, and a handful of his peers, conceptualized a distinctively American architectural style, reflecting the new social order and the ideals of democracy.

In the early 1800s, having attained independence only a few years earlier and having reaffirmed that independence in the War of 1812, Americans felt a camaraderie with the Greeks just beginning their war for independence from the Turks. Newspapers carried detailed reports of the war, as well as lyrical essays describing the Greek countryside and its noble ruins. It was during this time that Ithaca, Troy, and Syracuse, in western New York were settled. Parents hoping to inspire their children gave them names such as Diodates and Aristarchus. The study of classical poetry and languages was revived.

Public buildings were designed with classical motifs borrowed from the Greek temple, in what became known as the Greek Revival style. Ithiel Town's designs spread the style's popularity. Born in Thompson, Connecticut, Town acquired a fortune by engineering a superior bridge truss. His wealth secured, he settled in New Haven and devoted himself to architecture. It was in the use of Greek forms on domestic buildings that Town's work was most influential. Only in the United States did Greek forms ever appear in domestic architecture. The Russell house is an example of Town's early attempts to combine the form and decoration of a Greek temple with an interior suited to living and entertaining on a grand scale.

Town designed Russell House around a monumental portico of six Corinthian columns originally intended for the Eagle Bank in New Haven. Full-height columns, supporting a heavy entablature and a low pediment, gave the house the monumentality and magnificence of a public building. The exterior walls, constructed of wood with flush siding, were scored to resemble cut stone blocks. The interior was organized around a central hall with two rooms on either side, a plan which evolved in this country during the eighteenth century. Close attention to detail, not only in craftsmanship, but also in classical precedent, characterized the decorative treatment of the house, both interior and exterior.

The influence of Russell House can still be seen up and down High Street. Many of the houses built afterward draw faithfully on the vocabulary of Russell House, offering only a slightly more modest interpretation. Other houses constructed throughout Middletown, built for families of more modest means, exhibit only the low-pitched roof oriented toward the street, and a facade ornamented with pilasters and a cornice to suggest a pedimented temple. □

Middletown as a Pewter Center

Beginning in the 1750s, pewterers, silversmiths, and tinsmiths established shops along what was then known as Henshaw Lane. The lane had been laid out running west from Main Street in 1748. In 1753, Benjamin Henshaw, a West Indies trader, bought land on the north side of the new road, and built a home. (Benjamin Henshaw enlarged his original dwelling in 1777 by building a large gambrel-roofed Colonial house adjoining it. This structure still stands, at the northeast intersection of College and Broad Streets, and is presently occupied by Mazzotta's Restaurant.)

Thomas Danforth II, who arrived in Middletown in 1755, bought property on the north side of Henshaw Lane in 1759 between the homelots of Jonathan Yoemans and Benjamin Henshaw. Three months later, he opened a pewter and brazier (brass working) shop. Danforth was born in Taunton, Massachusetts, and apprenticed as a pewterer under his father, Thomas Danforth, in Norwich, Connecticut. He was soon joined on Henshaw Lane by several other artisans. Joseph King, the son of Capt. Henry King, set himself up as a silversmith in 1765 on land he inherited from his father's estate, at the northwest corner of

Pewter teapots were produced in large numbers between 1750 and 1800, but few examples still exist. Only three pear-shaped teapots credited to Connecticut pewterers have survived, including the one shown here. It has been attributed to either Thomas Danforth II, or Thomas

Danforth III. (The mark "TD" on the inside bottom of the teapot has led to discussions among experts as to which Danforth was responsible for the piece.) Thomas Danforth II was a craftsman in Middletown from 1756 until his death in 1782. Thomas Danforth III, apprenticed

under his father in Middletown, and then opened shop in Rocky Hill, Connecticut (then known as Stepney) in 1777. By 1800, this style of teapot was replaced by a taller form.
Courtesy New Haven Colony Historical Society

Main Street and Henshaw Lane. Property on the south side of Henshaw Lane was sold in 1756 to Samuel Winship, a skilled blacksmith. Over the next seventy-five years, other metal working shops were established by William Cleaver, Jr.; Jacob Whitmore; Amos Treadway, Jr.; and many others. There were also pewterers working outside the Henshaw Lane neighborhood, such as Jacob Eggleston on South Main Street, and Amasa Sizer in Staddle Hill, but "the Danforths on Henshaw Lane remained the focal point for the pewter production in the area." (Reynolds)

Prior to the American Revolution, England prohibited the exportation of tin, the primary element used in making pewter, to limit competition in the production of finished metal products. Pewterers and tinsmiths in America depended on old and broken housewares for their supply of metal. Even after American independence, pewter goods were recycled. In 1799, Elisha Barnes of Middletown advertised in the Connecticut Courant: "Cash paid for 5 or 6 cwt old pewter @ 10p per pound if delivered at Wm Danforth's in 40 or 50 days." Pewterers made utilitarian household products such as flatware, including plates and spoons, and hollowware, such as mugs and teapots. Pewter baby bottles, candlesticks, and chamber pots were also popular. The demand for pewter ware remained constant, even after England flooded the American market with inexpensive ceramic plates, bowls, and teapots following the Revolution. Pewter products had a higher status, even for basic household goods, enabling a large number of pewterers to stay in business to meet the demand.

Thomas Danforth II was probably attracted to Middletown because there were no other pewterers. In 1756, Middletown ranked as the most populated town in Connecticut, and was its leading riverport. The residents of Middletown provided a ready market for Danforth's pewter goods, and the people of nearby towns looked to Middletown for their supplies. Middletown was also the site of a lead mine, opened in 1775, near the banks of the Connecticut River, at the southern end of town. The lead mine provided Danforth with an accessible source of lead. "Lead from the Middletown mine may well have been used to extend or increase the yield of raw pewter from melted down pewter objects." (Reynolds) A study done by Charles Montgomery to determine the percentage of various metals in pewter objects from the late Colonial period, revealed that the Danforth pieces were higher in lead content than pieces from other pewterers in Philadelphia and New York.

Between 1756 and 1825, Middletown became home to 24 pewterers, ranking it with Boston (25), and Philadephia (40). Henshaw Lane, dominated by master craftsmen of the Danforth family, was the center of Middletown's pewter industry throughout this period. Intermarriage within the enclave, such as when Joseph King's sister, Elizabeth, wed Jacob Whitmore, a Henshaw Lane pewterer, helped unite the families and avoid competition. The artisans also shared expenses through partnerships. Before Samuel Hamlin moved his pewter business to Hartford, he had been a partner of Thomas Danforth. Two Danforth sons, Jonathan and William, also worked together for a time. Craftsmen often shared ownership of supplies, such as pewter molds, allowing them to keep costs down. Probably the most important ingredient to the success of Henshaw Lane as an artisan enclave, however, was the apprenticeship system. Rooted in old world guild practices, the apprenticeship system served to train new generations of artisans, as well as provide established craftsmen with labor in their shops. Thomas Danforth II trained five of his children as pewterers, who in turn took in several local boys as apprentices, including Samuel Pierce, James Porter, Stephen Barnes, and William Nott. After serving their apprenticeships, a number of pewterers relocated to other towns; for example, Samuel Pierce moved to Greenfield, Massachusetts. But most of the others became the third generation of pewterers on Henshaw Lane.

Thomas Danforth II produced large volumes of a wide assortment of items. The inventory of his estate lists twenty-eight sugar bowls and fourteen teapots, as well as about $4,000 worth of equipment for pewter production, and three carts used for trading his pewter wares. Danforth was "a talented and successful merchant, and the Middletown products were apparently marketed over a wide geographical range by direct shipments to merchants and peddler's wagon." (Thomas) By using the Connecticut River trade route and the roadways that fanned out from Middletown's center, Danforth, and other artisans were able to establish trade networks throughout the colonies.

After Thomas Danforth's death in 1782, two of his sons, Joseph and William, continued as pewterers on Henshaw Lane. Joseph built a house just west of his father's and operated his own shop until his death at the age of thirty in 1788. Samuel Hamlin also served an apprenticeship under Danforth, and in 1767 opened a pewter shop in Hartford, later moving to Providence. In Providence, Hamlin went into partnership with Gershom Jones, who had learned his trade with Thomas Danforth's brother, John, in

Norwich, Connecticut. Joseph Danforth's widow, Sarah, married Ambrose Seymour in 1793, and for several years he carried on Joseph's pewter business until the Danforth children came of age.

After 1825 there was a steady decline in the use of pewter for housewares, and Henshaw Lane gradually became a mixed commercial and residential neighborhood. In 1857, Henshaw Lane became College Street and the shops of former artisans were gradually replaced by brick commercial buildings, as well as Odd Fellows Hall (1839) and Middlesex Opera House (1892). On the north side of the street, the pewter shop of Thomas Danforth II was sold out of the family in 1866, and altered by the addition of an Italianate-style house between the shop and the street. During the twentieth century it was divided into apartments, and its contribution to Middletown's history was all but forgotten. While the Greater Middletown Preservation Trust was carrying out its

resource survey of Middletown's historic buildings in 1978, the Danforth shop was rediscovered, along with the home of Joseph Danforth, directly to the west. At the time, Farmers and Merchants Savings Bank was planning to demolish both buildings to increase its parking facilities. The bank, the City, and the Trust cooperated to carefully dismantle and store both buildings. Joseph Danforth's house was subsequently sold and rebuilt on a site on Long Island, and the city of Middletown purchased the Danforth pewter shop. On a spring day in 1984, the councilmen of the city of Middletown and members of the Greater Middletown Preservation Trust raised the frame of the pewter shop on its new foundation at the corner of Church Street and Pleasant Street, overlooking the South Green. Plans were underway to convert the shop to a local history museum, and although the City still owns the building, a lack of funds stalled the project in 1987.

❏

Judge Seth Wetmore, in 1746, built one of the finest Georgian-style mansions of his day. The interior is of exceptional sophistication, and the north parlor, shown here, is recognized by architectural historians for its decorative detail. The corner shell cupboard incorporates a sunburst pattern and the pilasters on either side of the fireplace are marbelized. The paint-ing above the mantel was done directly on the wood panelling before it was mounted. So exceptional is the parlor, that the entire room was dismantled and brought to the Wadsworth Atheneum in Hartford as a permanent exhibit to represent the finest in Georgian architectural detail. The Atheneum replaced the room in the Wetmore house with an exact replica from modern materials. Judge Wetmore served as deputy to the Connecticut General Assembly for forty-eight terms, and Judge of the Hartford County Court. The Wetmore family entertained such notables as Jonathan Edwards, Aaron Burr, and General Lafayette. Courtesy Wesleyan University Library, Special Collections and Archives

Dissenters broke from the established church in 1747 and formed a Strict Congregational Society. Later known as the South Congregational Church, their second meeting house, built in 1830, was located on the site of the present church. Courtesy Colonel C. B. McCoid

This fashionable residence which once stood on Ferry Street was built, circa 1750, for Capt. John Easton. This gambrel-type Colonial-period structure was a good example of an eighteenth-century Connecticut River merchant's house. From 1777 to 1818, the house belonged to Arthur Magill, who with his son founded the Middletown Manufacturing Company, the first woolen mill in Middletown to utilize steam power. The Easton-Magill House was torn down in the 1950s during urban renewal. Courtesy Phil Salafia

The American Revolution

Although trade came to a halt during the Revolutionary War, Middletown wharves were busy supplying war vessels. At least sixteen privateers from Middletown were licensed by the General Assembly to seize English ships and interrupt the enemy's supply lines. A handsome profit could be made after the sale of the captured cargo, sometimes as much as $200,000 per vessel, at a time when militiamen made less than $2 per month, plus a blanket. Often, the bounty was split, with six shares going to the captain, four to the first mate, two to the second mate, and one share each to the sailors. The owners also received a cut, usually equivalent to the shares received by the captain and first mate. Privateering, however,

was risky. The schooner *Eagle*, with several Middletown men on board, was captured by the British in 1779 and the crew were held prisoner for several months in New York harbor.

On the battlefield, several local men, including Col. Return Jonathan Meigs, Maj. Robert Warner, Gen. Samuel Holden Parsons, and Gen. Comfort Sage, distinguished themselves as military leaders. Farmers supplied beef and grain for the Continental Army and a local lead mine provided raw material for munitions. Middletown also quartered loyalist prisoners of war, including William Franklin, Tory son of Benjamin Franklin, and Johann Louis DeKoven, a Hessian soldier who later married a local woman. □

The Puritans left England to escape the authority of the Church of England, but many more Englishmen came to Connecticut Colony over the next one hundred years seeking economic, not religious, opportunity. The Church of England, or Episcopal Church, organized a parish in Middletown in 1750 and called it Christ Church. The first church, shown here, was built on the South Green in 1755. Although most Episcopalians in Middletown were patriots during the American Revolution, their ties with the Church of England created suspicion as to their loyalty, forcing the church to close its doors for a brief period. Today the Episcopal Church is the Church of the Holy Trinity on Main Street.
From Richter's History, with permission of the Church of the Holy Trinity

This center-chimney Colonial-period house was built by a wealthy sea captain, Theophilus Cande, circa 1760 on Newfield Street. The Bacon family bought the house in the mid-nineteenth century. In this photograph, Nellie (Crane) Bacon sits with her children, Charles and Jennie, in 1909 on the lawn of their house.
Courtesy Mrs. Charles Bacon

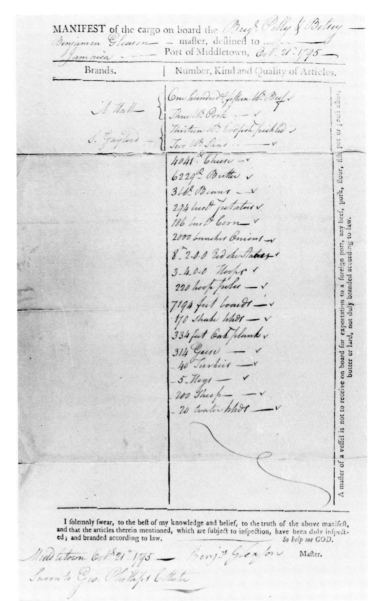

Benjamin Gleason, master of the brig
Polly & Betsy, submitted this manifest at
the Middletown Custom House before he
left for Jamaica in 1795. Middletown was
the official port of entry for the Connecticut River and each ship traveling upriver
was required to report its cargo listing at
the Custom House. Master Gleason ex-
changed the cargo in the West Indies for
rum, sugar, and slaves. He is listed on
the 1775 map as a slave dealer on
Middletown's Main Street.
Courtesy Connecticut River Museum,
Steamboat Dock, Essex

The establishment of the Strict Congregational Church and the Episcopalian
Church in the mid-eighteenth century
"pried open the door of toleration just a
bit wider." (Purcell, 1963) The Baptists
emerged as a dissident group who not
only renounced infant baptism, but also
openly criticized taxation by the Congregational Church. A Baptist revival in the
1780s and 1790s, resulted in the formation of Baptist societies in Portland, Middle Haddam, and East Hampton. In 1795,
members of the Strict Congregational
Church of Middletown were warned that
embracing the tenet of adult baptism by
immersion would result in involuntary
withdrawal from the church. Yet, it was
their pastor of seven years, Reverend
Samuel Parsons, who announced one Sunday morning that he embraced the opin-
ions of the Baptists. Upon his dismissal,
he and several of his former congregants
were baptized by immersion, and soon
thereafter, organized the Baptist Church
in Middletown. Before a small church
was built in 1811, the Baptists met in
various places, including a gristmill and
a carriage factory on South Main Street.
In the early 1840s, a Baptist revival
swept through Middletown, adding almost
one hundred members to the church, and
enabling the Baptists to build the present
church building in 1842.
Postcard, dated 1915, courtesy Larry
Marino Postcard Collection

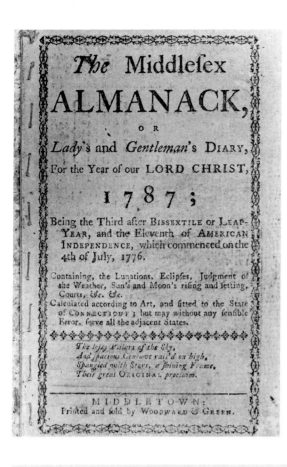

Middletown served as county seat after the formation of Middlesex County in 1785. A regional center, Middletown was home to publishers and printers. Thomas Green and Moses Woodward opened their printing office in 1785, and published the Middletown Gazette, Middletown's first newspaper. Woodward and Green went on to produce children's books, maps, and almanacs, such as the one pictured here. Courtesy Wesleyan University Library, Special Collections and Archives

Mansions of local sea captains, such as this home built for Benjamin Williams circa 1795, graced Middletown's riverfront during its years as a thriving trading port. Williams participated in West Indian trade as the owner of a small fleet of trading vessels. Henry L. DeKoven, a ship's captain, bought the house in 1818. Today, it is known as the DeKoven House and serves as a community center owned by the Rockfall Foundation.
Photograph, 1881, courtesy Rockfall Foundation

The brig American *was built in Haddam about 1816 and was mastered by Joseph Hubbard of Middletown. She was sold in 1818. Only a small percentage of vessels built in Middletown remained the property of local merchants. Most were loaded with trade goods and sold, with their cargo, in other ports. Many of Middletown's vessels became the property of merchants in New York and Nantucket.*
Photograph, from an 1820 painting by Antoine Roux, courtesy Connecticut River Museum, Steamboat Dock, Essex

Samuel Russell's 1828 mansion is nationally recognized as a major influence upon the development of the Greek Revival style in America. It was designed by Ithiel Town and built by Curtis and Hoadley of New Haven. Four generations of Russells lived in the house until it was sold to Wesleyan in 1936. It presently serves as the Honors College.
Photograph, circa 1920, courtesy Greater Middletown Preservation Trust, Anthony Hendrick Collection

Samuel and Frances Russell bought the entire block surrounding their house from Pearl to High streets and from Washington to Court streets. English formal gardens were laid out on the grounds and included boxwood imported from England and exotic plants brought by Russell from China. This 1920 view from Broad Street reveals the changes made to the house in 1855. At that time, the rear portico was enclosed and the double stairway of intricate ironwork was added. The two-story northern addition was also constructed and its design has been attributed to Alexander Jackson Davis, a former partner of Ithiel Town.
Courtesy Greater Middletown Preservation Trust, Anthony Hendrick Collection

The southwest parlor of the Samuel Russell House, circa 1920, exhibits careful attention to detail. The marble fireplaces are flanked by Ionic columns, and folding shutters are set into the recessed windows. A wide frieze and heavy cornice of decorative plaster define the high ceilings. Trompe l'oeil paintings simulate paneling in the north parlor, entrance hall, and stairwell.
Courtesy Greater Middletown Preservation Trust, Anthony Hendrick Collection

This typical children's book, printed by Moses Woodward in 1790, was owned by Jemima Gridley of Middletown. Children of the eighteenth century were treated as small adults. Books for young people trained them for their future roles in society. Although girls often received lessons in the three R's, learning piety and household skills was their chief educational duty.
Courtesy Wesleyan University Library, Special Collections and Archives

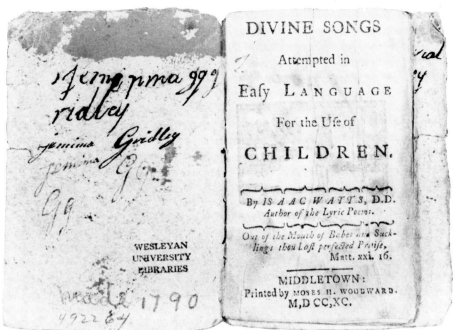

This house built for William Trench, at the corner of Broad and William streets, in 1839, is a fine example of the domestic Greek Revival style. Although it does not have large columns in front, it retains the basic temple form, with the gable facing the street. Instead of columns, flush pilasters were used at the corners of the house and surrounding the door. Geometrical patterns appear in the gable window and around the entry door.
Photograph by Matt Polansky

The Congregational Church built its fourth meeting house in 1799 on Main Street. Its design has been attributed to Lavius Fillmore, one of New England's most innovative architects of the late eighteenth century. Fillmore used one of his signature details, basket-shaped "lotus-form" capitals, to decorate the columns supporting the octagonal belfry. Fillmore was responsible for similar churches in East Haddam and Norwich, all of which used details such as beveled wooden quoins on the corners of the main block, as well as on the base of the tower, and a fanlight in the pavilion pediment. Until 1873, the Congregational Meeting House stood between the Custom House and the Middletown National Bank. This photograph was taken just before the church was moved to the north end of Main Street (next to O'Rourke's Diner).

According to local legend, the oxen were unable to turn the building around, therefore the rear of the church faces Main Street. In 1983, after years of neglect, the old church was renovated and the original facade (now at the rear), restored. Note, in the background, the present Congregational Church under construction on Court Street.
Courtesy J. Russell "Doc" Ward

Middletown Falls on Hard Times, 1800 to 1830

Trade promoted population growth and the incorporation of the city of Middletown in 1784. By 1790, Middletown was the largest city in Connecticut and the United States Customs port for the Connecticut River. Prosperity brought new problems to the city. Earlier New England society was rigid, and the family was assigned responsibility for those members falling on hard times. People without families looked to the town government to provide families willing to take them in. In this way not only the local poor, but the mentally retarded, the blind, and the elderly were cared for. Strangers who could not support themselves were "warned out" by Middletown officials and sent to other towns. As Middletown swelled with newcomers between 1750 and 1800, the family network failed. By 1800, support for the poor had become the largest expense in Middletown's budget, and in 1814 an almshouse was built on Warwick Street to board the local indigent. (From the 1930s until 1987 the building was home to the C. B. Stone Oil Company.)

There was no paid police force in eighteenth-century Middletown—none was needed. The family and church ensured order. After 1790, however, the city contended with drunkenness, thievery, and murder. A jail was added to the almshouse in 1846 for those convicted of lesser crimes; felons were expeditiously tried and hanged. Thomas Starr, descended from a long line of prosperous Middletonians, was hanged in 1797 for killing his cousin, Samuel Cornwall. Peter Lung met the same fate for the drunken beating of his wife in 1813.

President Jefferson's Non-Intercourse Act of 1807, also known as the Great Embargo, dealt Middletown's economy a death blow. Britain and France were at war, and American ships were being seized for the goods aboard and their crews were impressed into the British Navy. The embargo was passed in an effort to protect Americans and their investments. For two years, trade ceased, ships were moored in harbor, and there was no foreign market for surplus farm products. Young men looked for opportunity outside Middletown, many heading to western New York and Ohio. Old Middletown families completely disappeared from town, reappearing in places like Stow, Ohio, and Troy, New York. Only a few families who stayed prospered - and they, generally, made their fortunes in businesses located outside of Middletown; for example, Samuel Russell succeeded in the China trade and Charles Alsop made money on western railroad investments.

The Congregational Church was the official church of the state, and each person paid taxes for its support, regardless of his denomination. A national political conflict developed, between those who wanted the social order dominated by the Congregational Church to remain as it was (Federalists), and those who wanted to create revolutionary change (Jeffersonians). The Federalists held power in Middletown and fought to retain it by boycotting the businesses of Jeffersonians, refusing them credit and employment. Some Jeffersonians were arrested for criticizing Federalists.

At the center of the political troubles in Middletown was Joshua Stow. Born in Middlefield, he was appointed Middletown's postmaster and tax collector for his support of Jefferson in the presidential race of 1800. Stow made himself a target of the Federalist majority in Middletown in 1818, when he presented the motion at the Connecticut Constitutional Convention that ultimately disestablished the Congregational Church. In 1820

In 1853 the city bought the former home of Thomas G. Mather on Silver Street for the new Town Farm. Far from the "corrupting" influences of the city, the inmates farmed the land to earn their keep. The city used the Town Farm for the local indigent until the early 1920s, finally selling it in 1946. It later served as the McDonough Inn and the Town Farms Inn. In 1989, it was purchased for use as an alcohol and drug rehabilitation center.
Photograph by John Giammatteo

Convicted killers were induced to write confessions and apologies, such as this one by Lucian Hall, Betheul Roberts, and William Bell in 1844. These booklets were used by local ministers as cautionary sermons about the wages of sin.
Courtesy Wesleyan University Library, Special Collection and Archives

A MINUTE
AND CORRECT ACCOUNT OF THE
TRIAL
OF
LUCIAN HALL, BETHUEL ROBERTS
AND
WILLIAM H. BELL,
FOR
MURDER,
AT THE MIDDLESEX SUPERIOR COURT, CONNECTICUT, FEBRUARY TERM, 1844.

With the Indictment: Names of the Grand and Petit Jurors; the Testimony in full: the Charge of the Court to the Petit Jury: Addresses of Counsel: and the Sentence upon the Prisoner: with the Judge's Address to Him;
ACCOMPANIED WITH
PLATES AND CUTS
REPRESENTING THE HOUSE IN WHICH THE MURDER WAS COMMITTED: THE COUNTRY AND LOCALITIES BETWEEN THAT AND THE RESIDENCE OF
HALL:
SHOWING HIS ROUTE; WITH HIS
CONFESSION
SIGNED BY HIMSELF, AND A FAC SIMILE OF HIS SIGNATURE TO THE SAME;
AND A REPRESENTATION OF HIS
WOUNDED AND BLOODY RIGHT HAND:
And other Interesting Matters relating to the Murder and Trial.

he filed a libel suit in Superior Court against a newspaper editor who had branded him an "infidel." At the trial, virtually every Federalist in town, including Stow's brothers and sisters, testified to his "ungodly" behavior. Although victorious in his case, Stow was vilified for his involvement in Durham's Ethosian Society, a group of liberal thinkers who met to discuss the works of Enlightenment philosophers, and for his role in bringing ministers of other denominations to preach at Middlefield's Congregational Church.

In an effort to create jobs and lend Middletown social prestige, a group of concerned business leaders offered money and land to lure an educational institution to the city. After an unsuccessful attempt to persuade Washington College (later Trinity College) to locate here, Middletown settled in 1824 for Capt. Alden Partridge's American Literary, Scientific, and Military Academy. Partridge moved his school from Vermont into two buildings on High Street, today known as North College and South College of Wesleyan University. A man more concerned with money than education, Partridge did not live up to Middletown's expectations. In 1829 Partridge returned his school to Vermont and the Academy buildings were left vacant. Prudently, local businessmen retained control of the school funds and buildings, offering them two years later to Methodist churchmen who founded Wesleyan University. □

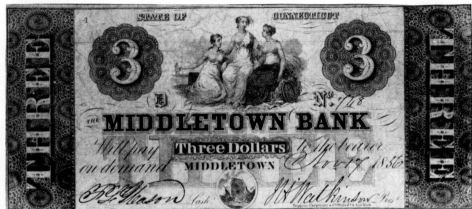

Bank notes, such as these issued by the Middletown Bank, were used in the first half of the nineteenth century. These bills were called "change notes," and were issued during periods when silver coin, the standard currency, was scarce. The Middletown Bank, incorporated under the national banking laws in 1865, was located on the west side of Main Street, between the Court House and the Congregational Meeting House, on the site presently occupied by the Connecticut Bank and Trust.
Courtesy Wesleyan University Library, Special Collection and Archives

Anne Royall, an English traveler through Middletown in 1828, visited Partridge's Academy and declared him "one of the most common clowns that ever undertook to keep a school." Of the academy she noted: "The halls and stairs were knee-deep in dirt and the boys, instead of being at their studies, were romping and squealing all through the rooms, up and down the stairs, nothing but loud talking and horse laughs." (Harrington)
Courtesy Wesleyan University Library, Special Collections and Archives

A portrait of Joshua Stow.
Courtesy Middlesex County Historical Society

The ability to harness water power transformed the nature of industry in the early nineteenth century. This dam on the Pamaecha River, photographed in 1870, belonged to one of the many textile and machine-tool factories located on that stream.
From the 1870 Class Album of William H. Peters. Courtesy Wesleyan University Library, Special Collections and Archives

2

The Revitalization of Middletown
1830 to 1860

❏

Business and Industry

It became clear in the 1830s that Middletown would never again be a major port; Middletown's young leaders, such as Samuel D. Hubbard and Samuel Russell, set out to revitalize the economy. Industry was targeted as the key to boosting Middletown's economy. Until 1790, England monopolized commercial manufacturing. The colonies supplied raw materials, such as wool and lumber, while England produced finished goods. Nonetheless, textile and weapon factories had been established in Middletown at the turn of the century, and beginning in 1830, the city enticed several new kinds of industries into the community.

One of the most successful industries of this period was the Russell Manufacturing Company begun in 1833 by Samuel D. Hubbard and Samuel Russell. Incorporated with capital from Russell's financial success in the China trade, the company did not begin to thrive until the 1840s, when Henry G. Hubbard, Russell's nephew, developed a method of weaving elastic webbing. This material was used for men's suspenders, and more importantly, for industrial belting to drive looms and lathes. Russell Manufacturing continued to be an industrial leader in Middletown for the next hundred years.

The Portland brownstone quarries were also profitable commercial ventures spanning the pe-

The manufacture of swords and firearms began in 1810 with Oliver Bidwell's firearm factory and the Simeon North pistol shop. However, the most successful factory was Nathan Starr's sword and pistol mill in Staddle Hill, established in 1812. A series of contracts with the govern- *ment, beginning during the War of 1812, kept Starr in business until 1845. Starr Mill was bought by the Russell Manufacturing Company, and it is shown here in 1880.*
Courtesy John Rzasa

riods of river trade and the new era of industry. Commercial quarries opened in the 1790s and provided building stone into the twentieth century. Brownstone was more easily quarried than granite because of its joints, or fissures, clearly visible in its sedimentary layers. The stone could be split along a joint by wedges and hammers, to produce appropriate-sized blocks that were dressed and finished. Portland brownstone was appreciated throughout the world for its rich color and fine grain. Builders created polychrome structures by combining Portland brownstone with other materials, an attractive and popular style of architecture presenting facades of varying colors and textures. Portland brownstone was used for many fine homes in New York and Philadelphia, and the stone was shipped around Cape Horn to San Francisco for the building of stately mansions.

During this period of economic revival, Irish immigrants arriving in Middletown were welcomed as a source of cheap labor desperately needed at the quarries, and in Middletown's factories. By 1850, the Irish constituted about one-quarter of Middletown's population.

As local churches diminished in importance as meeting places, public spaces were needed for business and social gatherings. Attractive hotels, with ample space for public meetings, were needed in Middletown if the growing city was to be a commercial center. Samuel Dickinson Hubbard, along with a group of investors, established the Mansion House in 1828 and the large Main Street building quickly became the focus of city life. The Mansion House covered most of the east-side block between William and College streets, incorporating a hotel and meeting rooms on the second and third floors, and businesses at street level. Middletown leaders often gathered in the meeting rooms of the Mansion House for important events, such as the founding of Wesleyan University. Other hotels were the Boardman House on South Main Street and the Central Hotel at the corner of Main and Court streets. □

John R. Watkinson, an English emigre, began the Pamaecha Manufacturing Company, a woolen mill on the Pamaecha River, in 1814. It was among the first of Middletown's textile mills of the nineteenth century, producing cotton and wool. Watkinson's mill building, shown here on South Main Street, was purchased by William Walter Wilcox and served as the offices for the Wilcox, Crittenden and Company until the 1970s. A local mason is presently planning to restore the 1814 mill building for his offices.
Courtesy Greater Middletown Preservation Trust

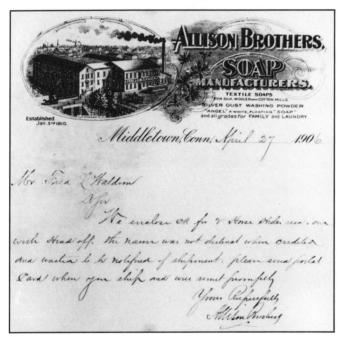

Allison Brothers Soap Works, one of the earliest businesses of its type in the country, relocated in 1810 from Hartford to Sumner Street in Middletown. It remained in operation until about 1920.
Letterhead courtesy Mrs. Helen Raffuse

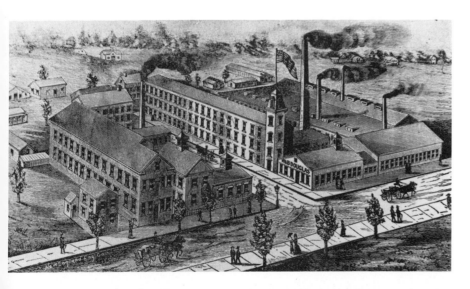

One of the first major industries enticed here was W. & B. Douglas Pump Works, in 1832. William and Benjamin Douglas found an international market for their "metallic pumps and hydraulic rams," produced at the southeast corner of Broad and William streets. This engraving of their operations is typical of the glowing images that illustrated local factories as busy and pleasant neighbors. The drawings of the factories often misrepresented their actual appearances, occasionally using fabricated drawings of nonexistent buildings.
From the 1896 Middletown Tribune Souvenir Edition, courtesy Mrs. Helen Raffuse

The William Wilcox Lock Company, founded in 1845 on the present Highland Avenue, employed up to 150 men to produce plate locks and padlocks.
Courtesy J. Russell "Doc" Ward

Wilcox Dam, at Highland Avenue and the Durham Road (today South Main Street), was used in 1870 as a source of power for the William Wilcox Lock Company, on the right.
From the 1870 Class Album of William H. Peters, courtesy Wesleyan University Library, Special Collections and Archives

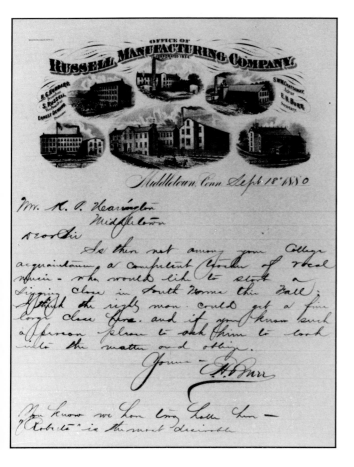

Nineteenth-century manufacturers were paternalistic. In Middletown, as this letter from the Russell Manufacturing Company illustrates, industrialists not only provided jobs, but sponsored educational and social services. Other manufacturers in town organized company bands, singing groups, and theatrical performances.
Courtesy of Ann Moskal Salonia

This photograph is probably of the Shaler and Hall Brownstone Quarry about 1880, located close to the river's edge in Portland. Quarrying and dressing of the stone were carried out primarily using hand tools with the aid of oxen and horses, until the 1880s.
Courtesy J. Russell "Doc" Ward

Portland was among the busiest ship-building communities in the state, building vessels at several yards in the Indian Hill section of town. Pictured here is the Freestone, a small schooner built in Portland in 1850 for transporting brownstone. It was lost at sea in 1896.
Courtesy Connecticut River Museum, Steamboat Dock, Essex

Steam-powered hoisting engines, cranes, and pumps facilitated the excavation of brownstone after 1880, and new techniques continued to be developed for the next twenty years. Railroad tracks were laid along the perimeter of the quarry to haul the stone to waiting ships, making beasts of burden obsolete.
Photograph, circa 1900, courtesy Colonel C. B. McCoid

MANSION-HOUSE,
E. W. NEWTON,
MIDDLETOWN, CONN.

The Washington Hotel, which stood at the southwest corner of Main and Washington streets, was built in 1812 on the homelot of Jabez Hamlin, Middletown's first mayor (1784-1791). In 1825, the hotel was the site of a reception for General Layfayette when he passed through Middletown on his way to the dedication of the Bunker Hill Memorial in Boston. After the hotel closed in 1835, it was home to Reverend Samuel F. Jarvis, the rector of Christ Church, and was occupied in 1860 by the Berkeley Divinity School. The building was torn down after the school moved to New Haven in 1928.
Courtesy J. Russell "Doc" Ward

The Mansion House was operated by a series of owners until it was sold in 1860 and renamed the Douglas House. In 1878, Anthony R. Parshley bought the hotel and called it the Clarendon House, and later the Forest City Hotel. After the building stopped serving as a hotel, it was referred to as the Mansion Block, which was torn down in 1978 and replaced by Metro Square.
Letterhead courtesy J. Russell "Doc" Ward

Institutions

The earliest colleges and universities in America were organized to train young men in ancient languages, philosophy, and literature, fields of study required particularly for entrance into the ministry. Harvard University in Cambridge, Massachusetts, and Yale Univesity in New Haven, Connecticut, were well-respected colleges that contributed to the prosperity of their respective communities. In the 1820s, Middletown sought the prestige that a respectable academic institution could lend. After the failure of Partridge's Academy in 1829, Middletown offered the Methodist Conference the abandoned academy buildings, plus a cash endowment of $33,333.33. The Methodists would contribute $66,666.66 to the school's endowment and permanently establish a college in the community based on Wesley's principles. All agreed to the terms, and classes began at Wesleyan University in September of 1831.

Several preparatory schools also opened in Middletown during this period. Although a majority of the city's youth attended public district schools, those with ambitions of attending college favored private instruction. Isaac Webb opened a school for boys on High Street in 1833, and Daniel Chase began the Middletown Institute and Preparatory School on Main Street in 1835. Girls could enroll in Dr. Chase's Female Seminary or Mary Ann Bartlett's school for girls.

The Berkeley Divinity School, associated with the local Episcopal church, was organized in 1854 as a seminary by Reverend John Williams, former president of Trinity College in Hartford. In 1928, Berkeley Divinity School moved to New Haven from the southwest corner of Main and Washington streets; in 1971 it officially became part of Yale Divinity School.

The *New Haven Journal*, on March 9, 1825, described Middletown's court house on Court and Pearl streets as "clumsy and decayed . . . it threatens to come tumbling on the heads of those who are within its reach." (Harrington) This courthouse had been built in 1786, soon after Middletown was designated as a seat of Middlesex County, alternating with Haddam on a monthly basis. In response to the criticism, the city undertook the construction of a new court house in 1832. It was built in the then-fashionable Greek Revival style on a prominent site on the west side of Main Street, in the block between College and Court streets. This block, which also included the Congregational Meeting House and the Middletown Bank, was chosen as the site for the new Custom House in 1834. When Middletown had been named a customs port in 1795, customs officials rented a small space on Main Street, and later moved to a brick building on the corner of Main and Washington streets. The new Custom House, also in the Greek Revival style, was large enough to handle the brisk business generated by industry. The addition of these new public buildings established this Main Street block as the center of the public life, and represented Middletown's confidence in its future growth.

In 1868, the Connecticut Hospital for the Insane was established in Middletown, on a picturesque site overlooking the river. The city had donated 158 acres of land to the state for the asylum. The hospital's dedication caused great activity in Middletown, with town residents participating in the festivities, and providing refreshments for the honored guests, among them the governor, members of the legislature, and Hartford city government officials. President Cummings of Wesleyan, in his welcoming address, outlined the attitude of society when he said, "It is the duty of government to protect the weak and to provide for the unfortunate and the helpless; the strong can care for themselves. No class is more dependent on public aid then those for whom this hospital is designed." (Ohno)

The concept that the mentally ill could be treated and cured was introduced in the early nineteenth century by Phillipe Pinel, a Frenchman, and William Tuke, an Englishman. Their philosophy, called "moral treatment," suggested that if removed from society, properly fed and clothed, exposed to fresh air, and given employment and exercise, the insane could be cured. Prior to this time, the mentally ill had been treated inhumanely, often relegated to workhouses or confined to prisons. Colonial society perceived the insane as victims of divine retribution. Moral treatment suggested that the mentally ill could best be treated at an institution far removed from the social conditions that were considered the cause of their illness. Urbanization during the early nineteenth century had caused significant overcrowding in many places, making it increasingly difficult to accommodate the mentally ill. Therefore, "moral treatment" appealed to a society anxious to remove the insane from the general population.

The Hartford Retreat (today the Institute for Living) was the first institution in Connecticut established for the moral treatment of the mentally ill. Built in 1824, the Retreat was a private hospital which quickly filled to capacity. In 1866, it was treating 202 patients, with at least 500 others waiting for a vacancy. When the population of Connecticut increased rapidly during the 1850s,

North and South Colleges looked like this in 1870. Originally built for Partridge's Academy, South College was the Wesleyan University chapel for many years and North College provided classrooms and dormitory space. North College was destroyed by a fire on the night of March 1, 1906. Within a year, the college rebuilt the present structure which is similar in appearance to the older one, except it is three stories instead of four. Today North and South Colleges are connected by a two-story addition, and house the university's administrative offices.
From the 1870 Class Album of William H. Peters, courtesy Wesleyan University Library, Special Collections and Archives

Isaac Webb opened a "Family School" for boys in 1833 on High Street, at the corner of William Street. Boys between the ages of ten and thirteen were instructed by Mr. Webb "to prepare them for admission to any college in the Union; or for mercantile or other pursuits." Rutherford B. Hayes was his most famous student. Wesleyan acquired the building for use as its first women's dormitory in 1889, and it became known as the "Quail Roost." It later housed the college bookstore and post office. Fire gutted the building in 1929, and it was torn down a year later.
Courtesy Larry Marino Postcard Collection

The Berkeley Divinity School bought the home of the Reverend Samuel F. Jarvis at the corner of Washington and Main streets (right), which earlier had been the Washington Hotel. The Reverend John Williams, founder of the school, resided on the first floor; classrooms and a library were located upstairs. The chapel (left) was built in 1861 for the divinity school. The buildings were demolished in 1928 and replaced by modern commercial buildings that have most recently housed J. C. Penney, Itkin's Decorators, and Connecticut Home Interiors.
Courtesy Middletown Press

and new industries bolstered the state's revenue, the legislation needed to found a state hospital for the insane at Middletown was passed. In 1866 land donated by the city of Middletown was chosen as the site for the new institution.

At the dedication in 1868, Middletown's contribution was recognized in an address by former Governor Joseph Hawley. "They [Middletown people] have given to the State, and to this work of humanity, 150 [158] acres of excellent land valued at over $30,000, and the Trustees purchased 80 acres more . . . The people of Middletown have built us a wharf, as you have seen, most convenient for all necessities. They have closed old highways and opened new ones." The board, which would oversee the administration of the hospital with the superintendent, was made up of twelve trustees, including three from Middletown, Benjamin Douglas, Julius Hotchkiss, and Dr. Joseph Cummings of Wesleyan. Middletown anticipated that the new institution would increase local employment opportunities, and lend prestige to the community.

Under its first superintendent, Dr. Abram Martin Shew, who served from 1866 to 1880, the early years of the Connecticut Hospital for the Insane were marked by optimism, family-oriented therapy, and traditional methods which characterized moral treatment. Patient lives were highly structured, with bells marking time for meals, physicians' rounds, and bedtime (7:30 P.M.). Fresh air and entertainment were essential ingredients in Dr. Shew's philosophy. In July of 1880, over half the patients, 225 people, sailed down the Connecticut River and into the Sound for a day at sea. Patients exercised, by walking and dancing, up to four hours a day. Religious services, musical and dramatic productions, and lectures helped occupy the patients' daily life. Those patients physically able were required to work on the farm or in shops on hospital grounds. The business activities on the farm reduced the cost of treatment. During the period of 1889-90, the hospital manufactured 2,085 brooms and brushes, 74 mattresses, 149 pairs of overalls, 65 pillows, 183 suspenders, and 12 rat traps, and 134 chairs were caned.

By 1872, when the state legislature required the hospital to care for the criminally insane, whom physicians viewed as incurable, there was serious overcrowding at the hospital. The chronically ill, who required long-term care, exceeded the number Shew anticipated. When the issue of overcrowding was discussed, Shew emphasized his philosophy that the institution should never be larger than that which could be handled by one administrator. However, the state owned extensive property at the Middletown site, and accordingly expanded the existing institution,

instead of building others elsewhere. To meet the needs of the hospital population, the cottage system was instituted through the purchase of residential buildings near the main campus for housing groups of patients with similar mental illnesses. Two houses were purchased south of the hospital in 1872, and cottages were established for chronically insane patients and unruly inmates. The carpenter's shop (now known as Stanley Hall) was refitted to house criminally insane patients. In 1876, with growth in the number of employees, sleeping quarters were provided for hospital workers. Although Shew had perceived the hospital as a place for treating and curing patients with mental diseases, by the 1880s the Connecticut Hospital for the insane was increasingly becoming a dumping ground for social outcasts, including epileptics, "idiots," and alcoholics. The hospital's emphasis gradually shifted from therapeutic treatment to long-term care.

Moral treatment of patients was reconsidered after Dr. Charles Page was named the superintendent in 1898. He reorganized the facility and redefined the hospital's role in society. Patients were regrouped into categories, based on the symptoms they exhibited, and patients within each group were uniformly treated. Although this more efficiently divided the labor of the staff, individual care was reduced to a minimum. Occupational therapy was increased and more domestic goods were manufactured and sold. Although the work required of patients was increased, they were not paid for their labor. The farm was enlarged, and greenhouses built. In 1900, the hospital harvested $21,000 worth of produce, which was sold to maintain the hospital. In 1944, the hospital farm grossed more than $95,000 through the sale of fruits, vegetables, eggs, dairy products, and livestock. However, as the costs of running the farm and workshops increased, they became less profitable, and were discontinued during the 1950s.

During the first several decades of the twentieth century, the hospital relied more on drug therapy and hydrotherapy. Physiological studies were made to better understand the internal causes of mental illness. After 1900 superintendents were hired for their bureaucratic efficiency, more than for their success rate in treating the mentally ill. A second state hospital, built in Norwich in 1904, did little to ease overcrowding.

Ways of treating the mentally impaired came under fire in the early decades of the twentieth century, primarily due to the book, *A Mind that Found Itself,* written by a former patient at the Connecticut Hospital, Clifford Beers. He chronicled the poor conditions and the brutish treatment he received at the hands of attendants during his

The Court House, built in 1832 on Main Street, stood between what is today Farmers and Mechanics Bank and Connecticut Bank and Trust Company. Middletown and Haddam, as the geographical centers of Middlesex County, were designated the county seats when Middlesex County was formed in 1785. Middletown built its first court house on Court and Pearl streets in 1786. While serving county business, each successive court house also served Middletown municipal needs. In 1893, the Main Street court house was torn down, and City Hall constructed on its site, which was owned jointly by the county and the city.
Courtesy Rushford Center, Inc., J. Russell "Doc" Ward Collection

The Custom House was built in 1834 by Barzallai Sage, a noted local builder. This structure was torn down in 1916 and replaced by the Post Office.
Courtesy J. Russell "Doc" Ward

Christ Church was located at Broad and Court streets before 1874. When Christ Church changed its name to Church of the Holy Trinity and relocated to Main Street in 1874, this building was purchased by Mrs. Frances Russell for Middletown's first public library. She spent $20,000 to make alterations in the Gothic Revival style to the 1834 building and dedicated the library to the memory of her husband, Samuel Russell.
Courtesy Wesleyan University Library, Special Collections and Archives

In 1892, the main buildings at the Connecticut Hospital for the Insane were surrounded by elegant gardens. The design of the building and grounds was crucial to the precept of moral treatment. Superintendent Shew hired architects Sloan and Hutton of Philadelphia to design the main building for the hospital, which was intended to meet all the needs of the institution. The building, of Portland brownstone, was 765 feet long, with a central pavilion for the chapel and superintendent's rooms, and three retreating wings on each side to accommodate 450 patients. The grounds were designed like a park, to create a peaceful mood, and to dispel the idea that the patients were there as punishment. Nearby Butler's Creek was dammed to provide a water source. Today the institution is known as Connecticut Valley Hospital (CVH) and includes eighty buildings, (although not all are in use), on over 650 acres. *From Parish,* Scenes of Middlesex County, *courtesy Greater Middletown Preservation Trust*

Connecticut Hospital for the Insane required its own wharf to land supplies needed for the construction of the buildings. The city of Middletown responded in 1866 by appropriating $800 for the purchase of the site for Asylum Dock, shown here about 1900. After completion of the hospital, the dock remained in use to receive provisions for the hospital, including the annual supply of coal. A coal shed, with a capacity for storing five hundred tons of coal, was built at the landing.
Courtesy Middletown Press

Connecticut Hospital for the Insane had grown in the twenty-five years since its incorporation from one main building (today called Shew Hall) on 158 acres, to four separate complexes on 466 acres in 1895. A list of patients in 1870, includes the suspected causes of their illnesses, such as intemperance, overexertion, epilepsy, exposure, religious excitement, business anxieties, death of a friend, disappointed affections, physical injury, ill health, sunstroke, paralysis, typhoid fever, inflammation of the brain, hereditary predisposition, syphilis, masturbation, fright, jealousy, tobacco, riotous living, and old age.
From Lucius R. Hazen's 1896 Views of Middletown, *courtesy Everett Wright*

one and one-half years as a patient. Due to his perception of the arbitrary attitude of doctors and the lack of therapy in mental institutions, Beers recommended that borderline cases be transferred to community hospitals and outpatient clinics. In 1909 he established the Connecticut Society for Mental Hygiene, which developed into a national movement aimed at improving the way mental institutions were run. By 1910 several of the Hygiene Society's recommendations were adopted, including provisions for outpatient treatment for newly afflicted persons so that they could avoid institutionalization, and follow-up care for patients recently discharged from mental hospitals. In the 1960s and 1970s, this same philosophy, along with problems with staff shortages and decreased funds, eventually led to deinstitutionalization of patients who were considered functional enough to care for themselves in general society. Since the mid-fifties, the hospital has been known as Connecticut Valley Hospital, and occupies 650 acres east and south of the original site. Over eighty

structures stand on hospital grounds, although only about fifty are presently in use. At the turn of the century there was a total of 1,752 patients. Today the number of hospital patients has decreased to 500.

In 1870, the Connecticut Industrial School for Girls, located at Long Lane, was founded by local citizens for the "guardianship, discipline and instruction of viciously inclined Girls between the ages of eight and sixteen." (1896 *Middletown Tribune* Souvenir Edition) The institution considered the girls victims of poor environments, who only required regular habits, pure air, and a wholesome atmosphere to improve themselves. The campus had a farm, box factory, and dressmaking department in which the girls worked and learned a trade. Educational facilities provided academic instruction, as well as lessons in cooking and sewing. When the girls completed their studies, they were placed with families that could further improve their moral upbringing until they came of age. □

In an effort to decrease damage from fires, an 1803 town ordinance required all residences and businesses to "keep in constant readiness and repair, one good leather bucket containing not less than two gallons" of water.
Courtesy Middlesex Mutual Assurance Company

Daniel W. Camp, Samuel Babcock, and Daniel W. Chase stand on the steps of the headquarters of Middlesex Mutual Assurance Company about 1882. Incorporated in 1836 as a fire insurance company, Middlesex Mutual built its headquarters in the Renaissance Revival style on Main Street in 1867. The company occupied the northern half of the second floor and leased the remainder to the People's Fire Insurance Company. The street level space was rented to Farmers and Mechanics Savings Bank and the First National Bank. The third floor was a hall for fraternal organizations.
Courtesy Middlesex Mutual Assurance Company

The growth of the city necessitated better fire protection, leading to the establishment of fire companies. The first efforts were begun in 1803, and by 1885, the town boasted four hose or hook-and-ladder companies. Since industrial fires were the most common disasters, several manufacturing enterprises, such as the Douglas Pump Works and the Russell Company, formed their own fire stations. Shown here in an 1865 photograph is the Hubbard Hose Company's hose cart with the northeast intersection of Main and Court streets visible in the background. Courtesy J. Russell "Doc" Ward

The Douglas Hose Company was housed on the east side of Main Street in the building with the large double doors adjacent to J. R. Pitt's Drugs and Medicine Store. The firehouse was three buildings south of Washington Street. The building on the far left was Jacob Steuck's bakery. This photograph was taken sometime after 1880, when Steuck bought the bakery, but before 1893 when he moved to the adjacent corner. To the right of the firehouse was the 1869 Fagan Block which housed William and Charles Fagan's real estate company, and after the turn of the century was the location of George Meech's grain store. The northern half of this building was demolished in 1939 to permit the construction of F. W. Woolworth's "5 & 10 cent store." The southern half of the structure most recently housed Vincent Amato's Toy and Hobby Center. The firehouse continued in operation at this site until the Central Fire Station was built in 1899 further north on Main Street. Courtesy J. Russell "Doc" Ward

The latest in firefighting equipment was proudly shown in front of the new Main Street firehouse about 1900. The Renaissance Revival style building, of brick and brownstone, was completed in 1899, and remains one of the North End's most distinctive buildings. In 1985, the Main Street firehouse underwent extensive restoration and modernization, and continues to service the community as the Middletown Fire Department Headquarters. Courtesy Middletown Press

51

When this engraving was done in 1850, the river was still a vital part of Middletown's transportation network, connecting the city to the rest of the world.
Courtesy J. Russell "Doc" Ward

Transportation

From the earliest days of settlement, the Connecticut River had linked Middletown with other towns. Sailing ships carried trade goods until the late nineteenth century, and successful commercial steamboat service began in 1822, when William C. Redfield of Cromwell started the Connecticut Steamboat Company, providing side-wheeler steamboat passage from Hartford to New York and thirteen points between. The service connected Middletown businessmen to major commercial centers in just fourteen hours, and those willing to pay for first-class accommodations traveled in fancy upholstered cabins. The voyages were not without risk, however; the boiler on the *New England* exploded off Essex in 1833, killing or injuring fifteen of its seventy passengers. One hundred and fifty people were killed aboard the *Lexington* in 1840 in the same type of explosion off Fishers Island in Long Island Sound.

Screw-driven steamers replaced side-wheelers in the latter half of the nineteenth century. These were subject to safety codes and boiler inspections, decreasing the risk of fire or explosion. The steamer's arrival in Middletown "was announced by a loud blast on the whistle to open the highway bridge and the railroad bridge." (Baldwin, 1968) "She came through the draw, a floating island of light and shimmering white. Sounds and movements seemed to merge—bells, shouts, the rattle of winches, people and hand trucks coming off and going on, all in a glare of light." (Dean Acheson, from Centennial Edition of the *Middletown Press*, 1984) Judge Raymond Baldwin, recalling his youth in Middletown, "thought it was wonderful to go to New York on the big boat" for his family's annual summer trip, and to visit his father's friend, Capt. Charlie Bacon of Middle-

town, in the pilot house. The steamers provided not only passenger service, but carried industrial freight to New York for nationwide distribution. The Russell Manufacturing Company and Wilcox, Crittenden and Company, for example, brought daily shipments to the freight house by the steamboat dock for the "roustabouts," or deck hands, to load onto the nightly steamer from Hartford to New York. Despite fierce lobbying by the owners of the steamship companies, the railroad emerged as competition for steamboat lines in the 1870s. Yet steamboat service continued until 1931. Today, cruise lines offer sightseeing excursions on the Connecticut River, including two-hour trips and all-day cruises to Long Island.

As early as 1835, Middletown investors discussed ways to connect Middletown to other urban centers by railroad. Their efforts culminated in the organization of the New York and Boston Railroad in 1846. Two years later a charter was granted by the state for a railroad bridge to cross the river at Middletown. Because the proposed railroad line would circumvent Hartford, the leaders of that city waged a legislative battle for the next twenty years to block Middletown's efforts. During that period, a branch line was laid from Middletown to Berlin (the New Britain and Middletown Railroad) and, in 1868, the Connecticut Valley Railroad connected Saybrook and Hartford with a depot at Middletown. However, under the leadership of O. V. Coffin, Middletown persisted in its efforts for a line from New York to Boston. Finally, in 1870, the Air Line Railroad began operation from New Haven to Middletown. Passing over steep and rugged terrain, the rail line required numerous viaducts and sharp curves—an engineering marvel. The bridge at Middletown, although a swing bridge and not the suspension

The ferry Brownstone is ready to load passengers on the Middletown side of the Connecticut River about 1900. Ferries began operation in 1726, soon after people settled on the east side of the river. By 1830, canoes and rowboats were replaced by flatbed ferries accommodating livestock and wagons. The toll was six cents for passengers and eight cents for a horse.
Courtesy John Irving Anderson Family

The Middletown ferry slip was located approximately where the bridges were built in 1896 and 1938. As this 1895 photograph illustrates, the ferry transported supplies as well as passengers.
Courtesy J. Russell "Doc" Ward

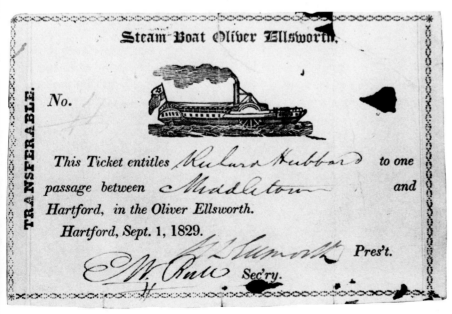

This is a ticket for passage on the steamer Oliver Ellsworth, a side-wheeler plying the waters of the Connecticut River beginning in 1824. Middletown was one of thirteen stops on its journey from New York to Hartford.
Courtesy Wesleyan University Library, Special Collections and Archives

The City of Hartford, *which served the area for twenty-three years, collided with the Middletown railroad bridge on March 29, 1876. The ship was owned by Hartford and New York Steamboat Company of Middletown. Although the* railroad bridge was open at the time, the fast-moving current of the river at flood stage drove the steamer into the bridge span.
Courtesy Rushford Center, Inc., J. Russell "Doc" Ward Collection

bridge originally proposed, was completed in 1872, connecting Middletown to Willimantic.

Although Middletown got a late start, the next few decades marked success for the Air Line, which spawned a significant increase in Middletown's industrial production. At this time, there were twenty-two railroads in Connecticut, totaling 868 miles of track. These lines competed for both passengers and freight. By 1900, the Air Line was losing business to the routes along the shoreline that avoided the bad curves and steep grades common on the Air Line route. Its problems compounded by the increasing use of the automobile, the Air Line discontinued its passenger express service. Through trains from New Haven to Willimantic stopped after World War I.

In its enthusiasm to obtain a major rail line, Middletown had committed $897,000 to the Air Line enterprise. When the line failed, it was a devastating blow to the city's economy. A bill, passed by the state in 1940, retired the debts still owed by Middletown and legislated that municipalities could no longer invest in railroad projects. The abandoned tracks of the Air Line later became part of the New York, New Haven and Hartford

Railroad. Limited freight service is now operated on the lines by the Central Connecticut Railroad.

Stagecoaches had provided passenger service since 1785, but roads were dusty, muddy, and frequently impassable. Overland travel improved in 1802 when the Middlesex Turnpike was completed from Wethersfield to Saybrook, today the approximate route of Route 154 (formerly Route 9A). But it was the streetcar, making its appearance in 1880s, that made Middletown's population mobile. Horse-drawn open streetcars carried passengers along Main Street to and from the railroad station. The 1890s brought electrically-powered trolley lines throughout the city and connected Middletown to Berlin, Hartford, and Meriden. Middletonians crowded the trolleys on their roundabout route to Ridge Road and Lakeview Park (now Crystal Lake); down Russell Street, to South Main; along Main Street to Grand, High, and Lincoln streets; and from Mount Vernon Street to Pine Street and Long Lane. At Lakeview Park the trolley company operated a pavilion and amusement hall, making it the most popular weekend retreat in town. □

The steamer Middletown was built in 1896 by the Columbia Iron Works and Drydock Company of Baltimore, Maryland. Powered with two 1,000-horsepower twin-screw engines, the Middletown cruised at 15 knots per hour. The ship held 350 passengers, who had a choice of different classes of cabins in which to travel. Steamboat service was available from Middletown to New York until 1931. Courtesy Middletown Press

To convince the state of the feasibility of a bridge, this rendering for a suspension bridge proposed in 1848 greatly reduced the actual width of the Narrows at Middletown. Despite Middletown's efforts, it was not until 1872 that a railroad bridge was built across the river at Middletown, completing the Air Line Railroad from New Haven to Willimantic. Courtesy Connecticut Historical Society

This photograph from Riverview Cemetery shows a Connecticut Valley Line train headed to Hartford, probably about 1880.
Courtesy Middlesex County Historical Society

This river scene was photographed from near the Middletown ferry landing, circa 1875. The railroad bridge, constructed in 1872, is in the background.
Courtesy John Irving Anderson Family

The Ghost Train at Middletown station. The Air Line Railroad operated this deluxe passenger train from 1891 to 1895. Painted white, with gold lettering, the Ghost Train made the run from New York to Boston in six hours, while passengers lounged in plush seats in the mahogany-paneled parlor car. On the day of its first run, schools were closed to allow the children to see its six cars whiz by.
Courtesy Wesleyan University Library, Special Collections and Archives

Train wreck in Maromas, 1911.
Courtesy Colonel C. B. McCoid

A local freight, heading south in the late 1940s, crosses Miller Street in Middletown's North End.
Photograph by Kent Cochrane, from T. J. McNamara Collection, permission of Quadrant Press

*The South Green trolley car, circa 1900.
Courtesy Richard and Mary Lou Goodrich*

*Trolley from Main Street to the Connecticut Hospital for the Insane, circa 1900.
Courtesy Richard and Mary Lou Goodrich*

*A drawbridge was built in 1896 to span the Connecticut River between Portland and Middletown. It crossed the river at approximately the same location as the ferry and the present Arrigoni bridge. This photograph of the bridge entrance was taken about 1920.
Courtesy Wesleyan University Library, Special Collections and Archives*

The African Methodist Episcopal Zion Church was built in 1830 on Cross Street, near the present site of Wesleyan University's Science Center. The building was remodeled in 1867 and, in the 1920s, was moved further west, to this site on Cross Street. In 1984 the church was razed and a new building constructed.
Photograph, circa 1978, courtesy of Greater Middletown Preservation Trust

Middletown's Black Community
The Era of Slavery

At least one-third of Middletown's families were directly or indirectly tied to the slave trade. Local sea captains carried slaves as part of the Triangle Trade. The Russell Manufacturing Company used thirty-one hundred bales of slave-picked cotton per year to weave cloth at its three mills and sold a large percentage of the cloth back to Southern plantation owners for use as clothing for slaves.

Some Middletown people owned slaves. The first Africans were brought to Middletown in 1661 via Barbados, and by 1756, 218 slaves were owned by a population of about 5,446 whites—at the time, the third largest black population in the colony. Slave dealing was a lucrative business. A typical newspaper advertisement announced the arrival of "The finest cargo of Negro men, women and boys" on a ship owned by John Bannister of Middletown in 1752. (Strother) Two slave dealers, Captain Gleason and Dr. Walker, advertised their offices on Main Street in 1775 and most of the merchants involved in West Indian trading also marketed slaves. Unlike the large plantation system that existed in the South, the pattern of ownership in Middletown was on a small scale. Few families in Middletown owned more than two slaves and they were primarily used as farm laborers or domestics. Slaveowners in Middletown were the larger land-owners and well-to-do ministers. By 1800 farmers whose sons had left to settle in the Western Reserves of Ohio and New York relied on black

labor to carry on their farming. As attested by the numerous notices in Middletown newspapers announcing rewards for runaway slaves, New England slaves were no more contented with their lot than their Southern counterparts.

When slavery ended in Connecticut by 1830, free blacks came to Middletown from rural regions, such as Colchester and Lebanon, in search of employment. Middletown was in need of labor, struggling to revive its economy after the decline of the river trade and the large population losses to the Westen Reserve, and therefore was receptive to newcomers.

In 1828 a group of local black men met at George Jeffrey's Cross Street home to organize a congregation of the African Methodist Episcopal Zion Church, the third of its type in the country and the second in Connecticut. The Reverend Jehiel C. Beman of Colchester, a shoemaker, was called as the first minister in 1831. During his tenure, the church became known as "The Freedom Church," and William Lloyd Garrison of Boston, abolitionist leader and publisher of the antislavery newspaper, *The Liberator*, was a frequent visitor. Beman's wife Clarissa found the Colored Female Anti-Slavery Society in 1834, only the second of its kind in the United States.

The Anti-Slavery Society

In the same year Jesse G. Baldwin, a white Middletown resident, was a driving force in the creation of the Middletown Anti-Slavery Society.

Benjamin Douglas, co-owner of the W. & B. Douglas Pump Works with his brother William, was an active abolitionist, yet was elected mayor of Middletown from 1850 to 1856 and lieutenant governor of the state from 1861 to 1862. During the New York Draft Riots in 1863 he rescued a runaway slave, Ephraim Dixon, from a vicious mob. Douglas smuggled Dixon out of New York and into Middletown and set him up in a barbershop on Main Street. The Dixon family remained in Middletown well into the twentieth century.
From Whittemore "History of Middletown," *in Beers* History of Middlesex County, *courtesy Greater Middletown Preservation Trust*

Born in Meriden, Baldwin came to this area in 1833 to open a store selling silver and plated ware. A peddler for many years traveling throughout the country, he had witnessed the horrors of slavery and determined to spend his life fighting it. When he expanded his business to manufacture cotton webbing, he used only cotton grown by free laborers. He sweetened his food with sugar that came only from "distant lands where there were no slaves" (Strother), and he even carried the sugar with him when he traveled.

The first meeting of the predominantly white Anti-Slavery Society was held at the Douglas Pump shop at Broad and William streets. (Baldwin's shop also was located on this block.) The pro-abolition speeches were barely underway when they were interrupted by a proslavery mob who threw stones and eggs into the windows. Even Mayor Elijah Hubbard could not deter the proslavery forces from attacking the abolitionists as they tried to escape.

Some of Middletown's most prominent businessmen and religious leaders risked their lives and livelihoods to take a stand against slavery, giving money and time to the cause. They opened their homes as safe houses to fugitive slaves along what was known as the Underground Railroad after the passage of the Fugitive Slave Act of 1850. Neither underground nor a railroad, the name for the network described the secrecy and the precision with which it carried out its work. After a brief stay in Middletown, slaves would move on to Wethersfield, Hartford, or Farmington, and then usually north to Canada.

Colonization

The first president of Wesleyan University, Wilbur Fisk, was one of the most outspoken advocates of the Colonization movement. Although Fisk agreed that the black slaves should be freed, he believed that there was no place for them in American society. In 1829 Miss Jane E. R. Watkinson of Middletown wrote to her cousin, Elijah Kent Hubbard at Yale University about the newly-formed American Colonization Society in Middletown. She believed that America and Africa would benefit from "the emancipation of our darkies and their colonization in Liberia." Hubbard, a liberal and free-thinking man, was appalled by her desire "to see this mighty mass of darkness rolled from our fair continent." (Elijah Kent Hubbard Collection, Wesleyan Special Collections) A group of Middletown blacks, headed by Jehiel Gilbert and Amos Beman (the son of the first minister of the A.M.E. Zion Church), condemned the Colonization movement with the resolution. "Truly, this is our home: here let us live, here let us die." (Rose & Brown)

A Small Population

In 1830 there were 208 Americans of African descent in the Middletown community. Because their names and occupations are recorded, we can learn where they lived, who they married, and how they were employed. They were day laborers on farms and at the riverfront; they were barbers and sailors. Yet, with few exceptions, they could not find steady employment at the growing num-

ber of manufacturing businesses in Middletown. By 1850 factories were hiring Irish immigrants and the population of blacks in Middletown had decreased to 149 people.

Today, only a few of the black families in Middletown, such as the Warmsleys, can trace their ancestors to nineteenth-century Middletown. Josiah Warmsley, who had lived in South Kingston, Rhode Island in 1785, was farming in Middlefield by 1822, with his two sons, Horace and George. In 1880, as most blacks were leaving the area for lack of work, several Warmsley men found employment at area factories. James Warmsley was a firefighter. The Warmsley homestead, on Farm Hill Road in the South Farms District, is still in the family.

The McArthur family can trace its ancestors to the turn of the century in Middletown, when Alex McArthur was listed in the city directories as working at the Goodyear Rubber Company. Two McArthur women living in his household on Vine street were also employed, one as a clerk at the James H. Bunce Company, the other as a typesetter.

The McArthurs resided in Middletown's largest black neighborhood, near the A.M.E. Zion Church on Cross Street. The small houses that line Vine and Cross streets were home to Middletown's working class black families, with names such as Jeffrey, DeForest, Dixon, Beman, Carter, Sullivan, and Powers. (This neighborhood now houses Wesleyan students.) A small black community also developed along lower William and

John Warmsley was a liveryman working on Center Street, at either the Loveland or Steele stables, when this photograph was taken about 1875.
Courtesy Pauline P. Warmsley and Family

Court streets in the late nineteenth century. Still other black families lived on the outskirts of town and worked as farm laborers. George Street is named for two black farm laborers named George who lived at either end of the rural street.

The black population in Middletown declined sharply beginning in 1860. With the influx of Germans, Swedes, Poles, and Italians over the next thirty years, blacks had more difficulty finding work. When the European migration into Middletown reached its peak in 1910, only seventy-three blacks remained in the community. By 1920 the number had dropped to fifty-three. The black men and women who helped shape Middletown during the nineteenth century found opportunities elsewhere. □

Isaac Truitt worked for Wesleyan University as the school's chimney sweep during the 1870s. Student rooms were heated by stoves and a sweep was needed to maintain them in working order. Wesleyan students selected the photographs they wanted in their personalized yearbooks, and this photo of Isaac Truitt was a popular choice. Truitt lived on Vine Street. From the 1870 Class Album of William H. Peters, courtesy Wesleyan University Library, Special Collections and Archives

A young Middletown man posed for this portrait at a photographer's studio about 1895. The photograph was discovered in the Warmsley family photograph album, which contained portraits dating as early as 1875. He remains unidentified. Courtesy Mrs. Herbert (Lillian) Warmsley

This photograph of an unidentified Middletown gentleman, taken about 1900, was also found in the Warmsley family album.
Courtesy Mrs. Herbert (Lillian) Warmsley

Gen. Joseph King Fenno Mansfield, Middletown's Civil War hero, died in 1864 at the Battle of Antietam. His heirs sold his home on Main Street to the Middlesex County Historical Society in 1959. From Whittemore "History of Middletown," in Beers History of Middlesex County, *courtesy Greater Middletown Preservation Trust*

Lucius Bidwell, from Middletown, a Union soldier in Company B, Fourteenth Infantry Regiment, was killed on May 6, 1864. More than 830 men from Middletown served in the Civil War, of which at least sixteen were members of the "Colored Troops" and ten were of the "Irish Brigade."
Courtesy Middlesex County Historical Society

After the devastating fire in 1907, Wilcox, Crittenden and Company rebuilt its forge at what is today the corner of South Main Street and Pamaecha Avenue. Employees lined up in 1924 for this photograph: Victor Knowles, foreman, stands on the left, and clerk Jim Hayes on the right. "It was smoky. It was hot. It was noisy," recalls William Batty, who worked as the advertising manager for Wilcox, Crittenden from 1930 to 1971. Most residents in South Farms can recall the deafening pounding noise from the forge that could be heard for many blocks even during the 1960s, when the forge was owned by the

North and Judd Company. In 1988, the forge was converted to Forge Square Apartments, providing eighty-one units of moderate-income housing. Courtesy Bill Batty

3

"The Forest City" Takes Shape
1870 to 1920

❑

Industry, Business, and Social Institutions

After the Civil War, the process of urbanization transformed Main Street from a residential to a commercial center. Main Street, reputed to be the second widest in New England, was flanked by columns of trees that gave Middletown its nickname, the "Forest City." By 1870, private homes began to give way to brick commercial buildings that housed stores, restaurants, banks, and small businesses, and the city of Middletown began to look much as we know it today. Residential neighborhoods sprang up throughout Middletown to house the industrial labor force which grew from five hundred workers in 1850 to nearly twelve hundred in 1860.

Among the important companies to develop during Middletown's period of industrialization was Wilcox, Crittenden and Company, founded in 1869. For over three-quarters of a century it was one of the largest employers in Middletown and helped shape the community's development. The roots of the company can be traced to 1849 when Eldridge H. Penfield, while working at a local sail loft, invented a metal grommet that reinforced the holes through which ropes fed to raise and lower sails. Prior to this time, grommets had been hand made of rope and needed constant repair and re-

Middletown was nicknamed the "Forest City" because of its many tree-lined streets within the city limits. Main Street was as well-known for its fine elm and oak trees as it was for its stores and shops. Although this photograph of Main Street, taken as early as 1865, is somewhat blurry, it clearly captures the shaded appearance of Middletown's commercial center. The photograph was taken from north of the intersection of Washington Street and the steeple of the South Congregational Church can faintly be seen in the background. The broad Main Street was without curbs, its edges lined instead with hitching posts and horse blocks. Courtesy Greater Middletown Preservation Trust

placement. After a few years in business with his uncle, Ira K. Penfield, Eldridge sold his share to William Walter Wilcox. After Wilcox bought out Ira Penfield and joined with a new partner, Joseph Hall, Jr., of Portland, profits increased and the company (now Wilcox and Hall) moved from its small factory at the corner of Church and Hamlin streets to the factory built by John R. Watkinson in 1814 on South Main Street.

It was through Wilcox's determination that the company prospered. Instead of relying on salesmen to market the product, Wilcox took to the road himself:

With trunks full of grommets, and tools to insert them, Mr. Wilcox started out with the determination to visit all along the coast to Halifax, Nova Scotia, showing the use and utility of the new metallic grommet, presenting a gross or two to those who could not be induced to buy. In this way the business became a success. (Beers History of Middlesex County, 1884)

In 1869, after Hall's retirement, Wilcox took in his brother-in-law, Albert R. Crittenden, and changed the name of the firm to Wilcox, Crittenden and Company. Over the next fifty years the company expanded, eventually producing over eight thousand specialized items for maritime use. By the late nineteenth century, the company had established an international reputation as a manufacturer of marine hardware and held an exclusive contract with the British Admiralty. The firm employed many German immigrants, as well as several black laborers, and strove to retain its workers on the payroll during the Depression in the 1930s.

William Walter Wilcox became a Republican state legislator for two terms, ending a thirteen-

year span of Democratic representation from Middletown. After his retirement in 1891, his son, William Walter Wilcox, Jr., became president, and upon Wilcox, Jr.'s death in 1940, William Wilcox III assumed control. In 1957, the company was bought out by the North and Judd Company of New Britain which merged with the nationwide operations of the Gulf and Western Company in 1968. North and Judd occupied the Wilcox, Crittenden buildings from 1968 until relocating to the Westfield Industrial Park in 1971. Since then the 1901 machine shop, along with its 1912 addition (opposite Warwick Street), has been converted to the Parker House condominiums, and the 1907 forge building is now Forge Square apartments. The 1814 Watkinson Mill, saved from demolition by the efforts of the Greater Middletown Preservation Trust, is presently being restored as offices by a local mason. □

Wesleyan University

During Wesleyan's first twenty-five years, the university remained in the two buildings on fourteen acres that it inherited from Capt. Alden Partridge's American, Literary, Scientific, and Military Academy. Not until the 1850s did the school achieve the look of a college campus, when, just before Joseph Cummings was inaugurated as president in 1857, it seeded lawns, planted trees, and laid out a baseball field behind North College and South College, the buildings that had housed the academy.

It was during President Cummings's tenure, 1857 to 1880, that Wesleyan University underwent its first important period of physical growth. He was responsible for the "brown old row of col

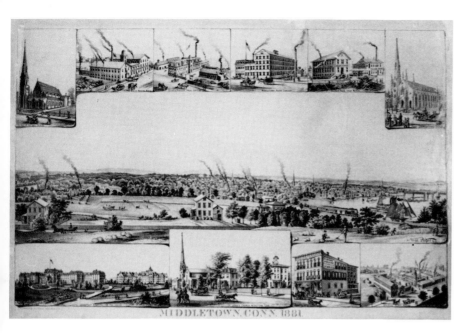

lege halls," (Price, 1931) that extends southward from North and South College, lending Wesleyan its distinctive character. The completion of Rich Hall library in 1869, allowed the university to move its book collections from the Lyceum in North College to a fine Gothic Revival style brownstone building. Named in honor of Isaac Rich, who pledged $25,000 for its construction, the building served as the university's library until 1928, when Olin Memorial Library was constructed. With the help of a gift from the class of 1892 Rich Hall was converted to a theater, the Class of 92 Theater.

On the day in 1869 when Rich Hall was dedicated, the cornerstone was laid for Memorial Chapel, just to the south on College Row. With the dedication of this new chapel in 1871, South College, which had been used for religious services, was converted to administrative offices. Designed by G. B. Keeting, Memorial Chapel was also a brownstone structure in the Gothic Revival style, incorporating pointed arched windows, steep gables, and a steeple tower with pinnacles. Thirteen stained-glass memorial windows commemorate the Wesleyan University faculty members and students who lost their lives in the Civil War.

Cummings also had Judd Hall of Natural Sciences built on the northeast corner of High and College streets and had the old Boarding Hall, south of Rich Hall, remodeled into Observatory Hall, complete with a tower equipped with a refracting telescope. Cummings owed his success in expanding the campus to the number of friendships he had cultivated with people who later made generous subscriptions to Wesleyan's endowment fund. He was also the first president

of the university who maintained good health throughout his tenure. Previous presidents, such as Wilbur Fisk and Stephen Olin, had spent many of their years in office combating ill health.

President Cummings's also introduced the practice of summer vacations, initially providing students with an eight-week holiday in the summer months, and later, eleven weeks, by shortening the winter and spring vacations. At that time, commencement was moved from the last week in August to early June. The most innovative changes during Cummings's tenure, however, were to the school's curriculum, accomplished through the faculty's efforts. The elective system was instituted, providing students with broader course offerings and the ability to choose the courses they wanted. Wilbur Fisk had proposed the idea in the 1830s, but the school's funds did not allow him to offer any courses beyond those needed for graduation. Between 1858 and 1869, the curriculum was enlarged, more professors were hired (five between 1871 and 1876), and advanced work in a number of subjects, such as science laboratories and modern languages, was offered. By 1872, three courses of study at Wesleyan were available: Classical (A.B.), Latin Scientific (Ph.B.), and Scientific (B.S.). Cummings, a conservative educator, viewed these radical changes with misgivings. When an economic depression jarred the country during the 1870s, the value of Wesleyan's once healthy endowment fund was seriously reduced. Cummings resigned his post in 1880.

Cyrus D. Foss, Cummings's replacement as president, solved Wesleyan's financial problems. During his inauguration, one speaker commented, "The age of stone, we trust, has past: the age of gold, we hope, has come." (Price) The era of the great brownstone buildings had passed; Foss's role was to renew the endowments, securing the financial future of the university. Where Cummings had ruled with "strict paternalism" (Price), Foss controlled the students with the force of his character, instilling in them a sense of right and justice. Discipline was shared between administration and faculty, and students were occupied with winning the approval of the faculty, instead of testing them with small infractions of the rules. But student pranks were common in the 1880s. The janitor's cow once appeared atop South College, and the chapel bell was plugged to silence the students' call to services. On another occasion, the chapel seats, smothered in glue, "refused to release some of the students when they tried to rise." (Price) Students sawed the legs on the altar benches halfway through, causing the faculty to crash to the floor during chapel.

The most famous campus ritual concerns the Douglas cannon. Since 1867, the brass cannon, measuring 23½ inches long and 5½ inches in diameter, has made a brief visit to the campus on February 22, or sometime within that week, then vanished to places unknown. The cannon was made for Company B, 169th Infantry Division of Middletown in 1867, and stored at the Douglas Battery, the division's armory. Soon after the cannon's arrival in Middletown, it was stolen by Wesleyan students. Although it was returned, it continued to be "stolen" each year on or about Washington's birthday. After the battery was torn down, the cannon was moved to a small brick building on William Street that was part of the W. & B. Douglas Pump Works. When the cannon was stolen in 1869, the thieves filled it with gunpowder, blowing out several windows at Judd Hall and causing one student to lose a few fingers. The administration made a rule that cannons could no longer be fired on campus. The ritual turned into a game—the freshman class would emerge with the cannon around midnight, and maintain possession by beating off attacks by the sophomore class. Since 1867, the cannon has been "disguised, imitated . . . buried, and drowned" in the Connecticut River. (Price) Its yearly emergence is not guaranteed; in 1916 it disappeared for almost fifteen years. When it resurfaced about 1930, it was mounted alongside the flagpole in front of College Row. An inscription was placed on its pedestal: "The Douglas Cannon—Born in obscurity—Reared in strife—Tempered by travel—Never discouraged—Home at last—October, 1931." Of course, it was not long before cannon-nappers removed it from its "permanent home," and it has routinely appeared, at least every four years. The cannon most recently appeared at the

inauguration of President William M. Chace in September 1989. Installed upon a new, supposedly tamper-proof mounting, it remained in place for twenty-nine days.

Architect Henry Bacon, who was responsible for designing Washington D.C.'s Lincoln Memorial, developed a design for the expansion of Wesleyan University's campus at the turn of the century. The university expanded south to Church Street, west to Foss Hill, and north toward Washington Street. Scott Laboratory (1903) and Olin Memorial Library (1928) were built on Church Street. Fayerweather Gymnasium (1894) was built at the north end of College Row, adjacent to Dennison Terrace (presently Wyllis Avenue) which had recently been laid out as a residential neighborhood for university faculty. Van Vleck Observatory was built atop Foss Hill in 1916. ☐

Middlesex Hospital

Col. Herbert Camp and his sister, Mrs. E. Hershey Sneath, donated their family home on Crescent Street for the Middlesex Hospital in 1904. On the same day that the hospital officially opened, Steve Shenski, a quarry worker at the Brainerd-Shaler and Hall quarries, hopped a quarry locomotive as a quick way home from work. While jumping from the train, he lost his balance and fell beneath the engine, crushing his leg. A local doctor rushed him to the new hospital, where Dr. John E. Bailey and Dr. Francis D. Edgerton amputated his leg. The next day's *Middletown Press* credited the new facilities with saving Shenski's life.

Enthusiasm for the hospital, incorporated in 1895, had been slow to develop. Donations taken at local churches for several years were modest, and townspeople criticized the first site chosen, at the lower end of Washington Street, because of its proximity to the river and railroad. (It seems most residents felt this land could be put to a more profitable use.) The donation by the Camps, as well as a $10,000 inheritance from Mrs. Henry G. Hubbard, solved the problem of the hospital's location and enabled it to purchase necessary equipment.

At the turn of the century, people associated hospitals with death more than with healing. In the first year of the hospital's existence, only 108 patients were treated, 60 receiving medical care, and 48 requiring surgery. Most treatment was at home, given by the family doctor. Patients who came to the hospital were either unconscious or unable to contact a family physician. Maternity care was still the domain of the midwife; babies were born at home. Patients at the hospital paid $25 a week for a private room and the right to

Wilcox, Crittenden and Company expanded its operations to include a projecting addition to the 1814 Watkinson mill, built in the 1890s, and a brass foundry in Mill Hollow, on Mill Street, in 1898. In 1901, the company built a large two-story, brick machine shop, and the 1814 mill was converted to office space for executives. About 1890, an intricate complex of wooden structures, shown here, was built upon brick and stone piers over Pamaecha Creek, in the ravine below the main offices, to house tinning and galvanizing operations. Water from the creek was used to power the machinery and as a coolant in the galvanizing process. *Courtesy Bill Batty*

On the night of July 30, 1907, fire destroyed the wooden forge buildings of Wilcox, Crittenden and Company. Although the original mill building and the 1901 machine shop survived, much of the enterprise collapsed in ruins into Pamaecha Creek. Hardware patterns and many of the company's records were destroyed. Within two years, Wilcox, Crittenden built a new forge on the west side of the creek, further south on Route 17, without having lost a customer or laying off any of its two hundred employees. In 1912, the company expanded again, adding extensively to the 1901 machine shop. *Courtesy Bill Batty*

Elmer Ely (left) was the last shipbuilder plying his trade along Middletown's riverfront. He started his enterprise in Middletown in 1882, and earned a reputation as a master craftsman. Although much of his business involved making rowboats and sailboats, he also built eighty-foot steam-powered pleasure yachts.
Courtesy Rushford Center, Inc., J. Russell "Doc" Ward Collections

unlimited visitations by friends and family members. Those in wards paid $7 a week, but were allowed visitors only on Tuesdays, Thursdays, and Saturdays, and only for two hours. This was a hardship, when the average hospital stay was thirty days. These rules were amended in 1905 to allow daily visitors.

The hospital grew steadily. A surgical wing had been added to the new hospital two months after it opened, and in 1908 training for nurses was established. The entrance requirements stipulated that a girl be between twenty-one and thirty-five and be "at least average height and weight." Agnes M. Wood was appointed the school's first superintendent. This school has since been named for Ona M. Wilcox, who graduated from the training program in 1925, and served as its director until 1970. Nurses lived in the Ackley House on Crescent Street until the Hendley Memorial Home was constructed in 1915.

Between 1904 and 1920, additional wards were built every few years, including one for contagious diseases, a children's ward, and a pavilion for X-ray equipment. As demands increased (in 1924, the hospital reached the milestone of accommodating one hundred patients at once), the housing available at Hendley Memorial Home

could not meet the need for added professional nurses. In 1930, the Bengston-Wood Memorial Residence for nurses was dedicated offering accommodations for fifty-seven more student nurses. Expansion of the hospital was delayed by the lack of construction materials during World War II, and in 1953 the South Wing was completed. It was during the public subscription campaign for the South Wing that the hospital added "Memorial" to its name. The continued need for more space led administrators to hire a hospital consultant firm in the early sixties to propose plans for future development. The firm recommended that the hospital relocate to a less congested neighborhood that would provide room for expansion. A site near the present Xavier High School was considered, but plans were halted when re-use plans for the present hospital could not be found. Instead, Middlesex added two more floors to the South Wing in 1963, and in 1968 the original Camp homestead was demolished to permit construction of a $12 million wing, which opened in 1971. Presently, Middlesex Memorial Hospital owns and occupies most of the former residential buildings along Crescent Street, as well as several on Pleasant Street opposite the South Green. □

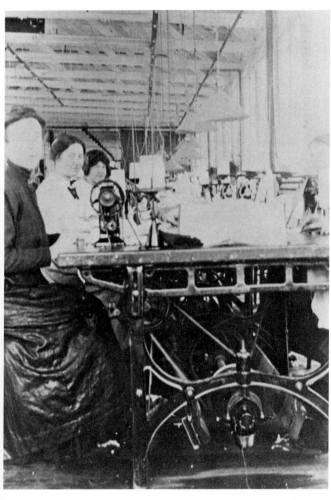

land has been asking, is 'Omo,' perfect in the absorption of perspiration, as well as wear and tear." (Penny Press) The company bought the factory of Stiles and Parker Press Company, and initially made a variety of rubber products. When the dress shields became their principal commodity, all other product lines were dropped.

Women ran sewing machines, but patterning and sales were male domains. Single girls, particularly from poorer families, would usually work until they married. Immigrant women usually found work in Middletown factories, supplementing their husband's income and enabling the family to move away from the crowded tenement neighborhoods. Women and children in the workplace were paid far less than men. For example, in a Waterbury brass mill, male assemblers earned $15.32 a week, in contrast to the $4.86 paid to women. Some men complained that the low wages paid women caused unemployment among men, but most felt that higher wages would lead to more women in the work force. Labor laws, after 1900, created better working conditions for both women and men, and limited to ten the daily hours worked by women. Near the turn of the century, factories were often visited by suffragettes who found that "the girls of the mills showed that they are awakening to the needs of the ballot." (Anderson, 1975) Miss Emily Pierson of Cromwell, a leader of the State Association for the Promotion of Women's Suffrage, was well received in Middletown.
Photograph, 1905, courtesy J. Russell "Doc" Ward

Women were hired to sew dress shields for the Omo Manufacturing Company, at the corner of River Road and Walnut streets, beginning in 1893. According to an 1898 article, "the name of the beautiful article, for which every lady in the

The former Union Mills building at the foot of Union Street was occupied by the Coles Company and is shown here in 1925. The oldest part of the mill, a two-story wing on the south side of the building (not visible in this photograph), served as a warehouse for West Indian cargo in the early 1800s. The Coles Company building was torn down for the construction of Acheson Drive (Route 9) in the late fifties.
Courtesy Northeast Utilities

The Coles Company, dealers in flour, feed, and grain, commenced business in 1898 in the former Union Mills building. George A. Coles, shown here in a company advertisement, had been in the grain business for thirty-five years, having worked at Union Mills beginning in 1862. After buying the Union Mills building in 1878, he operated several grain dealerships with various partners over the next twenty years. His partnership with his son, Charles H. Coles, led to the founding of the Coles Company. Their products were sold throughout the state. A deepwater channel to the mill, located at the foot of Union Street, allowed cargoes of grain to be brought in and fed directly into bins inside the mill. Bags of grain were then loaded onto railroad cars of the Connecticut Valley Railroad, whose tracks ran adjacent to the mill. All these tasks were mechanized, requiring minimal manual labor. George A. Coles also served as president of the Middletown Savings Bank and was active on Middletown's Board of Trade.
Courtesy Colonel C. B. McCoid

Penny Press To Middletown Press

When the forerunner to the Middletown Press, the Penny Press *was begun in 1884, it faced significant competition—the* Sentinel and Witness, *and the* Constitution, *both weeklies, and the* Daily Herald, *a daily paper like the* Penny Press. *Yet, the* Penny Press *became successful because it was blatantly a Democratic paper in a town dominated by Democrats, and it sold for only one penny (yearly subscriptions were $3). Within thirty years the* Press *emerged as the only survivor. The* Constitution *folded in 1890, and the* Daily Herald *succumbed in 1896. The* Sentinel and Witness, *owned by the same company as the* Press, *when it merged with the* Press *in 1899, stated, "Times change. The world moves. Great men go down in battle. Old and staid weekly publications cease to exist in the face of fierce daily competition."* (Middletown Press *Centennial Edition, 1984)*

The "fierce daily competition" for the Penny Press *was the* Middletown Tribune, *begun in 1893 as the Republican newspaper. After 1906 when the* Tribune *ceased operations, and except for a one-year run of the* Middletown Times *(1913-1914), the* Penny Press *had a monopoly in Middletown. When the price was raised to 2 cents in 1918, its name was changed to the* Evening Press, *and a year later, under new ownership, it became the* Middletown Press.

In 1784, Middletown's first newspaper, the Middletown Gazette, *was published by Moses Woodward and Thomas Green. In addition to news and advertisements, the paper printed sermons and morality stories. The* Gazette, *through a series of owners, remained in print until 1834. The* Middletown Press *can actually trace its ancestry to the* American Sentinel, *which was first printed in 1823. It merged with the one-year-old* Witness *in 1833, and became the* Sentinel and Witness *that was absorbed by the* Penny Press *in 1899.*

The Press *had its first offices on the east side of Main Street, one store north of Court Street. For a brief time it moved further north in the same block, but for most of the twentieth century it was located at 472 Main Street, on the east side of Main Street, north of Washington Street. In 1981 the* Middletown Press *moved to 2 Main Street and into its three-story modern headquarters designed by T. J. Palmer of Cobalt.*

Since 1959 the Middletown Press *has been owned by Woodridge and Russell D'Oench, brothers with extensive backgrounds in publishing. The* Middletown Press, *with over ninety-six full-time and seventy-four part-time employees, and contracts with over three hundred carriers, presently has a circulation of 21,000 and is read throughout the county. Over 6 million papers are printed yearly.*

When Richard Singleton took the position of Middletown's first police chief in 1870, he had no assistants and worked out of his brother's repair shop on Center Street. From 1882 to 1887, the police had their headquarters in the space on Main Street now occupied by Central News. As late as 1901, the police force consisted of only eight men. In this 1912 photograph, Chief Archibald Inglis (in the double-breasted coat) and Captain Joseph Kincaid (on his left) pose with their department in front of City Hall on Main Street where the police station was located. In 1943, a separate building was built for the police off Court Street, then behind the post office, where they remained until the present police station was purchased from the Vinal Technical School (formerly the Vinal Trade School) on Church Street in 1965.
Courtesy Anne Toczko Nowakowski

Joseph Cummings, president of Wesleyan University from 1858 to 1880, shaped the appearance of "College Row." This view of the Wesleyan University campus from Foss Hill shows the blending of old and new, as it appeared in 1870. From left to right: North College, South College, Memorial Chapel before its dedication in 1871, Rich Hall library, and Observatory Hall. The wooden structure set back behind the chapel and the library was the college barn. The area behind the campus was little more than a swamp until Andrus Field was created in 1897.
From the 1870 Class Album of William H. Peters, courtesy Wesleyan University Library, Special Collections and Archives

Wesleyan University built its first observatory in 1838 on Cross Street. It was replaced in 1868, when the old "Boarding Hall" adjacent to Rich Hall Library (today the Class of 92 Theater) was remodeled by the addition of an observatory tower to house a refracting telescope. The structure became known as Observatory Hall, fondly referred to as "old O. H.," shown here on a postcard dated 1912. The tower was removed when Van Vleck Observatory was built on Foss Hill in 1916, and "old O. H.," was replaced by Harriman Dormitory in 1928.
Courtesy Larry Marino Postcard Collection

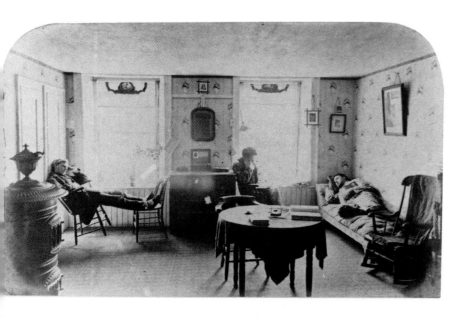

The boys in Wesleyan Room 38 lounge about their sitting room, complete with coal stove, in 1870.
From the 1870 Class Album of William H. Peters, courtesy Wesleyan University Library, Special Collections and Archives

Wesleyan University women students, 1891. When Wesleyan University admitted its first four women students in 1872, Bates College was the only other New England school accepting women. (Price, 1931) Between 1890 and 1900, Wesleyan graduated 157 women and about 600 men, creating fear among male students that, should the present rate of female enrollment continue, women would eventually dominate the institution. Owing to the hostile environment on campus, the trustees voted in 1900 to limit the number of women to 20 percent of the total student population. After 1909, women were no longer admitted at all, and in 1912, the last of the women graduated. The university did not accept women again until the 1970s.
Courtesy Middletown Press; permission Wesleyan University Library, Special Collections and Archives

The first high school in Connecticut was built in Middletown in 1840 on College Street (until 1974, Central School). A newfangled idea in its time, the high school established "grades" and prepared students for college. In 1849, boys and girls for the first time shared instruction in the same classroom. The town had a new Middletown High School built in 1895 (shown here). The Hartford firm of Curtis and Johnson designed the school in the Richardsonian Romanesque style and incorporated different materials, such as narrow Roman brick, brownstone, and terra cotta, to create a richly textured, polychromed effect. While asymmetry is suggested by the large octagonal tower, the plan of the building is organized around a central pavilion. Colonnades of narrow, two-story arched windows contrast with the three monumental arches of the entrance. Motifs are drawn from the work of the nineteenth-century architect, H. H. Richardson, but are based on medieval forms. No expense was spared to provide innovative luxuries such as central heating, separate bathrooms with modern plumbing, laboratories, drawing studios, and an auditorium. The school closed

in 1972, and in 1978 the building was converted to housing for senior citizens.

From Lucius R. Hazen's 1896 Views of Middletown, courtesy Everett Wright

The Middlesex Hospital opened in 1904 in what had been the home of the Camp family. A horse-drawn hack served as the first ambulance and was well-known in Middletown. The Literary Club (later the Middlesex Hospital Auxiliary) bought the rig for $543.22 to provide emergency transportation for patients to the hospital. William C. Manee stored it at his Rapallo Avenue stables and provided a horse, free of charge, for calls within the downtown area. Patients from outlying neighborhoods and towns were charged a regular taxi fee for the use of his horses to draw the rig. After World War I, the American Red Cross donated a motorized ambulance to the hospital.

Postcard, postmarked 1915, courtesy Mrs. Helen Raffuse

In 1924, the medical staff of the Middlesex Hospital stood on the steps of the main building for this photograph. Front row: Doctors Calef, Walsh, Murphy, and Mead; second row: Doctors Mitchell, Nolan, Kingman, Loveland, Hallock, Ives, Campbell, and Leak; third row: Doctors Burr, Harvey, Craig, Joyce, Wrang, and Chedel; back row: Doctors Whitney, Mountain, Sweet, Woodbridge, and Crowell. The two women doctors, Kate C. Mead and S. Mary Ives, were listed as consulting physicians for pediatric cases in hospital records; however, both are remembered as gynecological physicians in private practice. S. Mary Ives had joined the staff in 1920, but Mead was among the hospital's founders in 1904. Dr. Kate Campbell Mead had a private practice on Broad Street where she lived with her husband, William E. Mead, an English professor at Wesleyan University. At the turn of the century, Broad Street was often referred to as "Pill Alley" because of the many doctors located there. Doctors Mitchell, Calef, Loveland, and Kingman also lived and had offices on Broad Street. Doctor Mead was active on the nurse's Training School Committee and taught courses in gynecology. She was an ardent supporter of the women's hospital auxiliary, leaving the group $10,000 at the time of her death in 1950.
Courtesy Public Relations Office, Middlesex Memorial Hospital

Main Street

After 1870, Middletown's Main Street took on a new personality as families moved out into the surrounding neighborhoods and retail stores and commercial operations moved in. The stores, hotels, theaters, and restaurants lured people from all over Middletown and from neighboring towns in Middlesex County. Middletown's wide Main Street served as the major shopping center for the regional area. Judge Raymond Baldwin, who later became governor of the state of Connecticut, moved to Middletown in 1903 from Rye, New York, when still a young boy. Soon after he arrived, Baldwin was talking with a neighbor on Lincoln Street who asked him where his father had gone. When Baldwin replied, "He's gone down to the village," the man promptly corrected him. "Oh, your father hasn't gone down to the village. He's gone downtown." Baldwin quickly learned that "downtown" meant Main Street and the commercial district along the lesser roadways running east and west. Main Street had a South End and a North End, and three blocks in between. The public buildings were concentrated on the east side of Main Street, between Court and College streets, where the court and custom houses had been built in the 1830s.

By 1900, this block also incorporated City Hall and several banks. Judge Baldwin described Main Street at the turn of the century:
The street was paved with waterbound macadam. Waterbound macadam . . . is crushed stone rolled in with a steam roller. It presented a hard surface until the frost started to heave it. I've heard people say that in the spring there were holes [on Main Street] where a small horse could disappear. At that time there were a large number of elm trees along [Main Street] . . . It was lined and festooned with a number of telephone poles and telephone wires which increased in number and encumbrances as the years went by. There were two trolley tracks down the middle of the street . . . Main Street in those days ended at Crescent Street. For a number of years there was a tremendous movement that kept growing to extend Main Street right straight through . . . instead of turning down Union Street and then by Allison's soap factory . . . But Mr. Frederick King . . . one of the owners of Pelton and King Publishing Co. always appeared and opposed it . . . He wound up with the statement that 'God Almighty never intended that Main Street should extend beyond Crescent Street.' That sufficiently scared the [City] Council for a number of years . . . . (Baldwin's 1968 address to the Middlesex County Historical Society) □

77

This view of Middletown, taken in 1868 by Horace L. Bundy, is believed to be the first professional photograph of Middletown. It is taken from atop a building on the east side of High Street, between Court and College streets. To the right can be seen the first Middletown High School, which "somewhat resembled a barn with a cupola on one end." (Middletown Press Centennial Edition, 1984) H. L. Bundy began his photography career in Middletown with the firm Bundy and Burrows at 136 Main Street in 1865, and started his own business in 1868. Four years later he relocated to Hartford. Courtesy Wesleyan University Library, Special Collections and Archives

Main Street's North End

When Main Street was laid out, soon after the first settlers arrived, the proprietors chose its northern end for the core of their settlement. A fresh spring was nearby, and the ground was elevated enough to protect land from the yearly rising of the river. The meeting house was built near Main Street's intersection with the road to the spring (Spring Street) in 1652, and most families clustered nearby. Today, the only remnants from the earliest settlement are the brownstone graves in Riverview Cemetery. As the town grew and people scattered, the twenty-acre area north of Washington Street and east of the river became commonly known as the "North End."

During Middletown's first century, activity on Main Street shifted from the North End to the center and South End, where the majority of the residences also incorporated small shops or businesses. By 1776, according to Dr. Barratt's sketch of Main Street, the North End was sparsely populated, having only six property owners on the east side of Main Street. Among the inhabitants were two shipmasters and a ropemaker. The North End underwent tremendous growth during the nineteenth century. Here was where the two major railroad lines intersected and crossed the river by way of the railroad bridge. Union Railroad Station, built about 1878, created a great stir during the period when railroad transportation provided the fastest and most luxurious means of travel. Streetcars left the station in all directions to connect passengers to virtually all parts of town. Rapallo Avenue was opened as a public road in 1885, providing better access to the train depot. The road had once been Buttonball Lane, named for its rows of buttonball trees, and served as the lane to the Mortimer-Hackstaff Mansion built in the mid-eighteenth century. (The mansion was home to Capt. Philip Mortimer, an early Irish immigrant

who operated the ropewalk further south. When Capt. William Hackstaff bought the property near the turn of the nineteenth century he cultivated a tree-maze on the property between the house and Main Street.) The roads leading east from Main Street became crowded with tenements, home to the increasing number of immigrants finding their way to Middletown. By 1900, two hotels thrived in the North End—Glenshanan's Hotel, opposite the depot, and the Air Line Hotel at the head of Green Street—to provide accommodations for those arriving in Middletown by train. (The Air Line Hotel, later known as the Kingston Hotel, was destroyed by fire in 1967.) While the town's activities were concentrated in the North End, it underwent substantial development as brick commercial buildings, of three, four, and five stories, were built to house stores, offices, and apartments.

The majority of the Irish who found work in the Portland quarries and in Middletown factories lived in North End tenements built by local developers. Whether the "concentration of immigrants in the North End was the result of any sustained public or private policy" is uncertain, but by 1880, 30 percent of the population in the North End was made up of Irish immigrants. (Cunningham, 1985) This pattern of the North End serving as the first home for new immigrants continued. By 1920, more than half of the people residing on the side streets behind the commercial district on Main Street were from Melilli, Sicily. Today, as well, people of many races and national origins live in the North End.

Ferry Street, laid out in 1780, led to one of the town's ferry slips at the river's edge. Several houses on the street date from the Colonial or Federal period (1790-1830). These older homes were converted to apartments and boarding houses as the first immigrants arrived. The long tenement house at the foot of Green Street was built in the

With the increased demand for residential housing after 1870, O. Vincent Coffin, president of Middlesex Mutual Assurance Company and governor of the state, sub-divided several acres of land along Park Place soon after the street was laid out. He then sold the individual building lots to developers. This Second Empire style house, built circa 1875 by William H. Bishop, was the first in the new neighbor-hood. It still stands on Park Place, minus the large tower on the south side, and has been divided into apartments.
Courtesy J. Russell "Doc" Ward

Reginald deKoven, a Middletown native, gained national recognition as a songwriter and composer of operas in the latter part of the nineteenth century. He was born at the corner of High and William streets, in the house that had once been Isaac Webb's School. DeKoven composed several operas and hundreds of songs, but was best known for "O, Promise Me," which he composed as a young man in 1879 while living in Germany with his family.

Middletown offered a rich musical envi-ronment during the nineteenth century. Glee clubs were formed at Wesleyan Uni-versity and several of the churches, and the Middlesex Musical Institute provided enthusiasts with lessons in singing, instruments, and composition. With the opening of the railroads in the 1870s, Middletown was visited by celebrated en-tertainers, including the musical team of Ned Harrigan and Tony Hart. By 1900, the county had six theaters—among them the Middlesex Theater, MacDonough's Opera House, and the Goodspeed Theater —which offered live musical entertainment in the form of minstrel shows, operas, and dramas.
Courtesy Rockfall Foundation

Yearly flooding from the spring freshet did not deter early residents of Middle-town from building residential and indus-trial buildings close to the river's edge. However, most of the houses at the intersection of Union and Water streets, shown here in 1880, were built on tall foundations, or on piers, to decrease the damage from flooding. Union Mills, on the right, took advantage of its proximity to the river by carving a channel along its south elevation (not visible here) to allow boats to unload directly into the building. The houses at the lower end of Union Street were destroyed for the con-struction of the Route 9 overpass in the early 1950s. The only remaining part of Water Street, which once ran from Union Street to Bridge Street, serves as an entrance ramp onto Route 9 from the Harbor Park.
Courtesy J. Russell "Doc" Ward

The Leatherman appeared regularly in Middletown for over ten years in the late nineteenth century. Dressed entirely in leather, he walked a route that took him more than three hundred miles each year through New York and Connecticut, stopping at the same local residences for meals on each lap of his journey. Local legend claims he was Jules Bourglay, a Frenchman who fled France when spurned by his fiance. He had been responsible for the failure of her father's leather business in Lyon, and therefore, donned leather as a form of penitence. He never spoke, smoked a corncob pipe, and slept in caves along his route. He was known to avoid a house where too many questions had been asked on earlier visits. When this photograph was taken in Middletown in May 1888, he was showing physical signs of the mouth cancer that eventually claimed his life in Ossining, New York, one year later. Courtesy J. Russell "Doc" Ward

late-nineteenth century by Stiles and Parker Press Company to house many of its Italian laborers. (A similar tenement, torn down in the 1970s, had been built for workers of the Middlesex Quarry Company.) The houses at the upper end of the street were primarily built by Italian immigrants, including the three-deckers and the apartment blocks. The public school built on Green Street in 1872 was eventually bought by St. Sebastian Roman Catholic Church for use as a parochial school. Most recently it was purchased by Community Action for Greater Middletown (CAGM) for use as its headquarters. Edwin Netherwood, a carpenter/builder, developed Alsop Place, off Washington Street in 1898, advertising in the Middletown City Directory, "plans and estimates furnished free and homes built at cost." After the Hackstaff Mansion was torn down and replaced by Union Railroad Station, George Rapallo, an Italian immigrant from New York, built multi-family dwellings along the lane.

For most of the twentieth century, the side streets of the North End were lined with small businesses as well as homes. Marino's Bakery, on Ferry Street, and Pompey's Restaurant on Rapallo Avenue are two of the neighborhood restaurants that have survived. Until the 1950s, saloons, grocery stores, and florists catered to the needs of the neighborhood. Several families who owned businesses on Main Street also lived in the district. The Main Street firehouse, built in 1899, remains in use today.

The redevelopment programs of the 1950s and 1960s targeted the southern and central sections of Main Street. By the time the North End was considered for redevelopment, rehabilitation had replaced removal as the strategy for renewal, and the North End's integrity as a neighborhood has remained virtually intact. However, some buildings have been lost, and Gilshanen Place and Cherry Street were removed when DeKoven Drive was extended north from Washington Street to provide an alternative route to the North End, parallel to Main Street. Since 1978, the city of Middletown has made the preservation and revitalization of the North End a high priority. □

Portrait of an unidentified local man, about 1890, from the Warmsley family album. Courtesy Mrs. Herbert (Lillian) Warmsley

Broad Street was photographed looking north toward Washington Street in 1896. The center-chimney Colonial-period house on the right side of the view (which today houses Mazzotta's Restaurant) faces College Street, which intersects the center of the photograph. Randolph Pease built the house on the left in 1835, orienting the house so that it did not face either street. Pease, who owned a large dry goods and grocery establishment, built his first home on the northwest corner of College and Broad streets in 1822. When the city widened College Street to his front steps, he had this new home built with its back to the street in protest. The home was purchased in 1916 by the Church of Christ, Scientist, which removed the portico from the south side and replaced it on the north, thereby reorienting the house to face College Street. From Lucius R. Hazen's 1896 Views of Middletown, *courtesy Everett Wright*

81

When local boys left to fight in the Spanish-American War in 1898, Governor O. Vincent Coffin (right), a Middletown resident, was at the Union Railroad Station to see them off. Middletown was at the height of its industrial prosperity in the late nineteenth and early twentieth centuries, and many young men felt that their fighting the war would help guarantee the status of the United States as a world power.
Courtesy Middletown Press

A trainman for the New York, New Haven, and Hartford Railway Line (NY,NH, & H) takes a break with a friend at Union Railroad Station about 1900. After the decline of the Air Line Railroad and the Connecticut Valley Line, beginning about 1900, the New York, New Haven, and Hartford Line bought up most of the track and continued passenger service into the 1930s. Limited freight service is still provided by Connecticut Central Railroad, Inc., along the line from New Haven to Middletown. Since 1971, the Valley Railroad Company of Essex has been working to resume passenger rail service from Essex to northern towns, possibly to Middletown, along the Connecticut River. At present, their Connecticut Valley Line runs from Essex to Deep River as a tourist attraction.
Courtesy J. Russell "Doc" Ward

At the turn of the century, Middletown's waterfront was crowded with tenements. This photograph appears to be taken from near the foot of Ferry Street looking north toward Union Station. The houses on the right faced Water Street which ran along the river's edge.
Courtesy Rushford Center, Inc., J. Russell "Doc" Ward Collection

The low-lying neighborhoods close to the river suffered yearly when the spring freshet reclaimed the streets, as seen in this photograph, circa 1905, of the Sumner and South Street area. The years from 1900 to 1940 provided Middletown residents with valuable lessons about the damage that could be done by river flooding. Flooding in 1927 and 1936, as well as the flooding created by the hurricane of 1938, forced hundreds of families to evacuate with their possessions. As part of the urban renewal projects, retaining walls were built along the river, and low-lying areas were filled.
Courtesy J. Russell "Doc" Ward

Before kindergarten classes were provided by public schools, Miss Georgianna Minor operated preschool classes at her home on High Street, near the corner of Lawn Avenue. On the front stoop in 1907 (back row, left to right) are unidentified, Alice Shaeffer, Paul Shaeffer, unidentified, Elizabeth Nicolson, Georgianna Minor, and Teddy Acheson. In front with hat is Otis Hubbard. The Colonial period house is presently owned by Wesleyan University and is known as the German House.
Courtesy Middlesex County Historical Society

Taft Day was declared in 1909 when the president visited Middletown. Thomas MacDonough Russell draped his High Street house in bunting to celebrate the occasion. The Georgian Revival style house was designed by Russell, an architect and civil engineer, in 1901. Russell was mayor of Middletown from 1908 to 1909 and became president of the Russell Manufacturing Company in 1916. After he inherited the Samuel Russell House across the street, he sold his own home to Wesleyan University in 1934. A thirty-room addition to the west side was built twenty years later, when Wesleyan converted the house into a dormitory. The building is now the Center for Afro-American Studies.
Courtesy Robert Chamberlain

Anna Warmsley, the wife of Herbert Warmsley, Sr., worked as a cook for many years at Wesleyan University. Her husband was employed by Wilcox, Crittenden and Company in the late nineteenth and early twentieth centuries. The Warmsleys resided on the Durham Road (South Main Street) in South Farms.
Photograph, about 1910, courtesy Mrs. Herbert (Lillian) Warmsley

East Main Street, looking north from the intersection of Chestnut Street, was the residential hub of the South Farms district when this photograph was taken in 1915. Referred to at the time as Main Street, it connected Sumner Street with South Farms, before Main Street Extension was built in the 1930s. This part of the neighborhood was residential, made up of one- and two-family homes, belonging primarily to people of German and Irish descent. On the right, was St. John's Evangelical Lutheran Church (later Grace Lutheran), established in 1901. The Reverend F. W. Hassenflug lived in the house just north of the church. The neighborhood also included a saloon, a junk dealer, and a drug store. Further south on East Main Street, at the intersections of Elm and Baer streets, was the heart of the South Farms business community. Many German- and Irish-owned commercial enterprises were located here, including E. F. Reinsch's and J. A. Popps' barbershops, two shoemakers, Mr. Tynan's blacksmith shop, and F. P. Schram's grocery store. Saybrook Road was later built through this busy commercial center. *Courtesy Anne Toczko Nowakowski*

The International Order of Red Men (I.O.R.M.) was represented in Middletown by the Arawana Tribal Council, established about 1897. A national fraternal society, the Red Men immersed themselves in what they perceived as the culture of Native American tribal groups. Their leaders were given titles such as sachem, keeper of wampum, and chief of records. They dressed in Indian clothing and made weekend encampments to experience Indian life. The Red Men posed on the South Green, circa 1920, for this photograph. Women formed their own tribe, the Pocahontas Council, about 1903. *Courtesy Dorothy Clark Dickinson*

85

The Main Street block between College and Court streets was dominated by public buildings including the Middletown National Bank, the Congregational Meeting House, the Custom House, and the McDonough House, shown here before 1873. The Middletown Bank was the city's first banking institution, beginning in 1801, in the basement of Nehemiah Hubbard's house on Main Street. In 1813, the bank built a brick building at this site on Main Street with bank facilities at street level, and living quarters on the second floor. In 1855, the brick building was replaced by this brownstone structure. The name was changed in 1865 to the Middletown National Bank when the corporation was reorganized under the national banking laws. When City Hall was built next door in 1893, the bank was significantly remodeled to update its appearance. During the nineteenth century, many of Middletown's leading merchants and industrialists served as officers of the bank, including Joseph Alsop, Samuel Dickinson Hubbard, Henry L. DeKoven, and William W. Wilcox. Many of the same people that established the Middletown National Bank helped organize the Middletown Savings Bank in 1825 (now Liberty Bank for Savings) and the Middlesex County National Bank in 1830. Middletown's economy was rebounding during this period, and revenues from customs, manufacturing, and quarrying warranted several banking institutions. By 1900, Middletown had at least six banks located on Main Street. Middletown National Bank built the present building on the site in 1917, which now serves as a branch of the Connecticut Bank and Trust Company.
Courtesy Greater Middletown Preservation Trust

This has become a popular photograph of the Custom House because of the "disappearing dog" in the foreground. When this was taken, about 1875, photographers worked with large box cameras and film that required long exposures to register an image. In studio photography, subjects were often held in place by braces for the required time. While several of the subjects in this photograph held their pose throughout the exposure, the dog, which entered the scene midway through the exposure, registered only a ghost of an image.
Courtesy of Wesleyan University Library, Special Collections and Archives

The photographer was standing about where Thomas McDonough's house was on Main Street (presently Bob's Stores), circa 1875, looking south toward the South Congregational Church. Court Street crosses through the center of the photograph. The Congregational Meeting House had been removed in 1873 from between the Customs House (on the right, at the corner of Court Street) and the Middletown National Bank. Construction of the Shepard Block soon began on the former site of the meeting house. On April 9, 1873, the new building collapsed, killing six workmen and injuring sixteen others. At the inquest, the owner, Charles Shepard, Jr., was blamed for taking shortcuts in construction and starting the foundation when the ground was still frozen. It was not until 1880 that a building, the Bank Block, was finally constructed on this site.
Courtesy Wesleyan University Library, Special Collections and Archives

From the time of its construction in 1851, until after the turn of the century, the McDonough House was the leading hotel in Middletown. It was located at Main and Court streets until replaced by the present Liberty Bank for Savings building in 1928. The hotel's opera house provided entertainment such as minstrel shows, musical productions by Ned Harrigan and Tony Hart, a popular writing team, and speakers such as Susan B. Anthony and Henry Ward Beecher. With the advent of motion pictures, the opera house was converted to the Nickel Theater. Kids paid a nickel to see a silent movie, then headed to Lincoln's Drug Store, also in the McDonough House, for an ice-cream soda. These were popular gathering places for students heading home from the high school on Court Street.
Photograph, circa 1890, courtesy of the Greater Middletown Preservation Trust

When this photograph was taken in 1875, from Main Street looking east, Center Street was home to working class families, two livery stables (Henry S. Steele advertised his livery and hack services as being the "second below Main Street"), Oldack's saloon, Mackey and Williams blacksmith shop, and Hayden's grocery. Center Street was laid out sometime after 1800, connecting Main Street with Bank Street, and by 1825, it had become a quiet, residential neighborhood of nine houses, owned for the most part by members of the Hubbard or Southmayd families. After 1812 and the decline of the river trade in Middletown, Center Street residents turned their attention to banking, politics, and retailing, and gradually sold off their property and moved to more stylish neighborhoods west of Main Street. Retail businesses had for many years been located at Center and Main streets, including Lemuel Storrs's dry goods business at the southwest corner (opened 1811 on land he bought from John Southmayd), and on the opposite corner, the housewares store of Nehemiah and Richard Hubbard (circa 1800 to 1835). The Hubbards were also involved in local corporations; Nehemiah served as president of the Middletown National Bank, and Richard, his son, was on the board of directors of the Middlesex Mutual Assurance Company. After Richard's death, his wife sold the land to Elijah Loveland, who built a new barn in 1850 and established his thriving livery stable (seen here, on the left), originally in partnership with John Hayden. The old Southmayd homestead was the last lot to be subdivided, when Alfred Southmayd sold the family's property at the northeast end of the street to three parties: James Murphy, a tailor; John Schnieder, a shoemaker; and Frank S. Hills, a clerk. The old homesteads were converted to tenements for workers, and absentee landlords neglected the properties until the entire street was in disrepair. It was razed in the 1960s to make way for Riverview Center, a shopping plaza. Courtesy J. Russell "Doc" Ward

Looking down College Street from Main Street, circa 1875, the home of Governor Coffin stands on the left. In 1800, the lower end of College Street (known as Parsonage Street until 1857) was a residential neighborhood, much like Center Street and other nearby roads running from Main Street toward the river. Because College Street provided the most direct route to the steamboat dock, several commercial enterprises were at the east-

ern end of the street. During the fifty years between 1825 and 1875, the homes of the early families were converted into tenements for working-class families who were laborers in local factories such as Russell Manufacturing and the New England Enameling Company. Many of the landlords, including Stephen and Joseph Taylor, also owned interests in wharves and boat shops along the river. George W. Harris was one of the few

homeowners who continued to reside at his College Street property. Harris, a clerk at the Central National Bank, left an estate of almost $60,000 in 1888, as well as two houses on College Street. By 1890, Polish families dominated the street, particularly the lower end near the river, commonly referred to as "Duck Hollow," because of its frequent flooding. Courtesy J. Russell "Doc" Ward

In 1896, the southern end of Main Street still had many residential buildings. The Federal-style home of John R. Watkinson, built in 1810, is visible at the far right of this photograph. In 1919, the state of Connecticut bought the house for use as an armory and turned it to face south. A duplicate structure was built facing it and a drill shed was joined to the east wall of each wing. The National Guard still uses the building as its armory. The mansard-roofed building at the southeast corner of William and Main streets, opposite the 1842 Baptist Church, was the home of the Middletown Savings Bank from 1860 until it moved to the corner of Court Street in 1928. When this photograph was taken, Samuel Russell (grandson of the China merchant) was president of the bank. On the northeast corner of William and Main streets was C. A. Pelton's Drug Store, which opened in 1800 and is still in operation on the adjacent corner.
From Lucius R. Hazen's 1896 Views of Middletown, *courtesy Everett Wright*

This view was photographed, circa 1880, from Main Street looking east down Washington Street toward the river. The bakery of J. P. Hoffort occupied the southeast corner (on the right). The 1720 Gaylord House (on the left) was the Burnham Tavern from 1750 until about 1840—a popular meeting place for Middletown organizations, including the Freemasons and the Middletown Temperance Society. It was torn down in 1914 by the owners of J. W. Steuck's bakery to make way for Stueck's Modern Tavern. Later the building was bought by the Veterans of Foreign Wars (VFW).
Courtesy Wesleyan University Library, Special Collections and Archives

The same corner at Washington and Main streets was captured the morning of March 15, 1888, under about twenty inches of snow. The Blizzard of 1888 buried Middletown in twenty-one inches of snow from March 11 to 14. Hurricane-force gusts blew drifts up to ten feet high, immobilizing Middletown and major cities along the Eastern Seaboard. Jacob W. Steuck had bought Hoffort's Bakery (right) from his brother-in-law, J. P. Hoffort, in 1880. Steuck, a German immigrant, in 1893 moved his establishment into the four-story building he had constructed on the adjacent corner. At the turn of the century, he advertised his "Fancy and Domestic Bakery—Confectionery—Ice Cream—and Dining Rooms; Weddings and Parties Supplied."
Courtesy Greater Middletown Preservation Trust

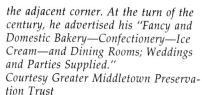

The Middletown Union Railroad Station, about 1910, at the foot of Rapallo Avenue. At this station, one could catch a train headed for Hartford, New York, New Britain, Willimantic, or Old Saybrook. Trolley lines from virtually any point in the city, as well as Meriden and Berlin, converged at Middletown's railroad station. Hotels for visitors to the city were available nearby, including the Air Line House across from the station.
Courtesy Colonel C. B. McCoid

As clean-up from the Blizzard of 1888 began, this boy and man on Court Street, outside the McDonough House on Court Street, are dwarfed by the towering snow piles.
Courtesy J. Russell "Doc" Ward

Commodore Thomas McDonough, the hero of the Battle of Lake Champlain, built this house in 1819. It stood just north of the hotel named in his honor, which stood at the northwest corner of Main and Court streets. When the Y.M.C.A. was organized in 1877, it bought the house and converted it to the facilities for its new organization.
Courtesy J. Russell "Doc" Ward

The Y.M.C.A. razed the Thomas McDonough house in 1893, and built a new facility on the same site, shown in this 1900 photograph. The "Y" had an active membership of 2,900 members in 1903, when about 25,000 people lived in Middletown. When the Y.M.C.A. moved to new quarters at Union and Crescent streets in 1928, the Sears and Roebuck Company bought this building and significantly remodeled it. Today, the building, much changed, is occupied by Bob's Stores. Courtesy J. Russell "Doc" Ward

To "contribute to the artistic development of Middletown," the Middlesex Mutual Assurance Company built the Middlesex Opera House in 1892. (Middlesex Mutual Assurance Company's Centennial, 1936) A few days after the opera house's dedication, fire destroyed the interior. It reopened five months later, its balconies and box seats decorated in murals and lavishly detailed plaster relief work. The Middlesex Opera House presented musicals, concerts, operas, minstrel shows, and vaudeville shows. The minstrel show was among the most popular forms of entertainment in the late nineteenth and early twentieth centuries, and contributed to the development of vaudeville and musical comedies. Minstrel entertainment was staged by white performers in blackface, who told jokes and caricatured blacks by singing songs in southern dialects.

In 1899, William Gillette, a playwright and actor, made Sherlock Holmes into a stage character and brought the play to the Middlesex stage. Gillette personified the brilliant fictional detective and repeated his performance time and again until his death in 1937. His success from Sherlock Holmes enabled him in 1911 to build a stone castle on 184 acres in Hadlyme, encircled by a miniature railroad.

In the late 1920s, the Middlesex Opera House was converted to a motion picture theater. The theater's flamboyant interior was removed in 1927 to make way for the movie screen and increased seating. Vacant for many years, the Middlesex Theater was torn down in 1980. Today the Opera House Restaurant occupies the former theater lobby.
From the 1896 Middletown Tribune Souvenir Edition, courtesy Mrs. Helen Raffuse

Until City Hall was constructed on Main Street in 1893, city business was conducted in the court house formerly on this site. The City Hall was a massive structure, made of Portland brownstone and built in the Romanesque Revival style. Also known as Richardsonian Romanesque, this style was extremely popular in the late nineteenth century for civic buildings. At the turn of the century, City Hall was one of Middletown's greatest landmarks, noted for the clock housed in its tower. Every day at 6:00 A.M. and 6:00 P.M., the clock would strike eighteen times, to emphasize the beginning and end of the work day. Butler's Insurance Company advertised its location as "opposite the town clock," so customers had no trouble finding it. In this 1900 photograph, City Hall was decorated in bunting and streamers as part of the city's 250th anniversary celebration. In 1961, when the building was less than seventy years old, it was torn down. At a time when most things old were considered obsolete, the leaders of government desired a more modern facility for the municipal offices, one that would accurately reflect their expanding vision of Middletown's future. In 1958, the Municipal Building was built at its present site, in the "Court Place Project Area," overlooking the Connecticut River and Route 9.
Courtesy Patrick Shugrue

Jacob Stueck moved his bakery and dining rooms across Washington Street into the first floor of the commercial block he had constructed in 1893. The building offered apartments on the upper floors. In 1914, Phillip Steuck, Jacob's son, bought and razed the Burnham Tavern on Washington Street to build Stueck's Modern Tavern, an addition to the Main Street bakery that offered a variety of dining rooms, as well as a ballroom on the third floor. The addition is visible on the far right side of this 1935 photograph. Stueck's business steadily declined after World War II, and the bakery and tavern were closed in 1949. Vision Corner has owned and occupied the building since 1977. Vision Corner is the largest provider of optical services and products in the Greater Hartford area.
Courtesy Vision Corner, Inc.

The Japanese Room of Steuck's Modern Tavern, circa 1920. Phillip Stueck, who built the tavern addition to the bakery started by his father, bought the Luther Briggs mansion at the northeast corner of Washington and High streets for his home. His widow resided there until her death in the late 1960s.
Courtesy Colonel C. B. McCoid

Mitchell's store, on the east side of Main Street, in the block between Center and College streets, sold merchandise ranging from curtains and rugs to clothing and cigars. Thomas F. Mitchell, the proprietor, closed the store in 1885, and left Middletown for Massachusetts.
Photograph, circa 1880, courtesy of J. Russell "Doc" Ward

Freshly killed game hangs in front of the Smith and Bishel store about 1900. Each year the Chafee Hotel held a game dinner, and because most of the guns and ammunition for the hunt were purchased at their store, Smith and Bishel displayed the kill. They opened in 1899, selling hardware, farm equipment, and feed in the Bank Block, next to the Custom House. Arthur Bishel, the son of a German immigrant, became the sole owner and moved the business across the street in 1924. The present store was built in 1961 and remains in the Bishel family.
Courtesy Smith and Bishel Company, Inc.

95

By 1910, when this photograph was taken of the Custom House, at the southwest corner of Court and Main streets, its services were no longer necessary. For twenty years after Middletown was designated, in 1795, as one of Connecticut's four customs ports, the region's prosperous trade network with the West Indies and Europe made the first Custom House on Main Street a busy place. All ships headed for towns along the Connecticut River, were required to show a cargo manifest at the Custom House. In 1832, trade was still such a vital part of the city's economy that it warranted the construction of this new brownstone Custom House. Even after the town's focus shifted from trade to industry, the Custom House saw enough activity from steamer freight service and, later, train service, to enable it to function through the nineteenth century. After 1892, immigrants arriving in Middletown by steamboats directly from Ellis Island, were required to register and have their possessions searched here. In 1916, the federal government, which had owned the site since 1841, decided to raze the building and use the site for a new post office.
Courtesy J. Russell "Doc" Ward

Two blocks on the east side of Main Street, between Court and William streets, do not retain any of the buildings that were standing when this photograph was taken in 1910. Governor O. Vincent Coffin's elegant mansion graced the corner of Main and College streets in the midst of a thriving commercial neighborhood. Governor Coffin, the first Middletown resident to fill the state's chief executive office, was elected in 1894. The Republican candidate won by the largest margin of any gubernatorial candidate in Connecticut's history up to that time. Coffin was born in Mansfield, New York, in 1836, and came to Middletown in 1864 as president of the Farmers' and Mechanics' Savings Bank. Beginning in 1884, and throughout the period when he was governor, Coffin served as president of the Middlesex Mutual Assurance Company. A man of seemingly infinite energy, he also held many other offices: director of the First National Bank; director, secretary,

and treasurer of the Air Line Railroad Company; president of the Y.M.C.A.; and mayor of Middletown. Governor Coffin's home was bought in the mid-twentieth century by the Benevolent Protective Order of Elks as their lodge building. A sign at the extreme right of the photograph advertises Yee Wak Laundry next to the Crescent Theater. At one point in the late nineteenth century, there were at least si Chinese laundries in Middletown.
Courtesy J. Russell "Doc" Ward

This 1773 center-chimney Colonial-period house on Court Street housed several businesses in 1910, when this photograph was taken. James D. Young, the son of a Scottish immigrant who started a small print shop on Cross Street in 1885, bought the house in 1922. The Colonial house was razed to make room for Young's bookbinding and printing business. The company is still operating on this site. Courtesy Young's Printing

When this photograph was taken, in 1919 at the north end of Main Street, M. J. Fitzgibbons was undoubtedly doing well in his bottling business. He was among the minority of local businessmen who owned a truck. In 1924, the advertisement for his Coca-Cola Bottling Works at 11 Rapallo Avenue included a telephone exchange, a luxury many other businessmen did not have at the time. In addition to Coca-Cola and mineral waters, Fitzgibbons bottled and distributed Arawana Ginger Ale, Hires Coco-Cola, and Nugrape. The Coca-Cola Bottling Works plant stayed in the Fitzgibbons family until the 1960s, moving to North Main Street, and then South Main Street, where it stands today. Courtesy J. Russell "Doc" Ward

James H. Bunce came to Middletown in 1856, and within nine years he had opened his own dry goods store and married Mary A. Hubbard, the daughter of one of Middletown's most prominent businessmen. With the addition of sixty-five thousand square feet to the original building, Bunce's became Middletown's first modern department store and the largest such enterprise in Middlesex County. Bunce hired immigrants and blacks when few retailers considered it, and he practiced innovative sales techniques, such as building a house on Pine Street to display furniture in a domestic setting. After Bunce's closed in 1974, Shapiro's department store occupied the location until 1986. It has since been divided into a retail mall, the Clocktower Shops, with offices on the upper floors. Photograph, 1940, courtesy J. Russell "Doc" Ward

In 1920 Harry and Rose Shapiro posed with their children, Sylvia, Muriel, Virginia, and Nathan, outside their Hubbard Street home. Harry's father, Joseph Aaron Shapiro, came to Portland in 1896, having been forced to close his saloon in Poland when the Czar decreed that only gentiles would be allowed to serve alcohol. After working at the Eastern Tinware Company for a few years, Joseph Shapiro became a peddler as he had once been in Poland. After more than ten years of selling dry goods door-to-door, he opened a store on Sumner Street under the name of J. A. Shapiro. When his son Harry Shapiro (pictured here) joined him in business, J. A. Shapiro and Son moved into a store in the former Mansion Block where Metro Square stands today. Several of Harry's children, including his son Nathan, joined them at the store In 1975, when the Mansion Block was razed, Shapiro's moved into the vacated James H. Bunce Company building, where it carried on business until 1986. *Courtesy Mrs. Max (Muriel Shapiro) Schulman*

4

Middletown Immigrants and Neighborhoods

❏

Ethnic Groups
The Irish

Many American cities were hostile to the large number of Irish who arrived between 1820 and 1850, denying them employment and housing. Yet Middletown welcomed the Irish immigrants. The primary reason for Middletown's hospitable attitude was its need for cheap labor to help accomplish the economic revival initiated after the decline of the river trade. Still, it is important to understand that "the immigrant population, while large, never constituted more than a quarter of the whole population ... Thus they were never the political threat to the established order in Middletown that they were elsewhere. They never over-taxed the ability of the marketplace to take them in as workers, nor did they constitute a significant drain on the community's charitable resources." (Hall, 1981)

The Irish were the first non-English immigrant group to arrive in Middletown in significant numbers. Immigration from Ireland came in several phases, and the immigrants represented several classes within Irish society. Those who came to Middletown before 1820 were primarily Protestants, and many had left Ireland because of the Trade and Navigation Acts imposed by Britain denying Irish the right to participate in industry and

St. John's Parish built this church, their second, at the northern end of Main Street in 1852. A house to the left was torn down in 1887 to make way for a new parochial school.
Courtesy Middletown Press

commerce. The Magills, Caseys, and Mortimers, who came to Middletown in the late eighteenth century, were of this group and were received quite favorably. The second wave, between 1820 and 1845, brought mostly southern Irish Catholics, who found work at Portland's brownstone quarries. The establishment of the Black Ball line of sailing packets in 1818 provided regular service from England to New York, costing 7 pounds (about $35), enabling working class Irish to avail themselves of economic opportunities in America. The Great Potato Blight in Ireland, from 1846 to 1848, brought large numbers of Irish to Middletown and Portland, constituting the third wave of Irish immigration, which continued until about 1900. This group differed from those that came earlier in that they were poor farmers, with little or no education, forced to flee desperate economic conditions.

Irish Catholic immigrants usually worked at Portland's brownstone quarries when they first arrived. By 1850, Portland, then part of Middle-

town, was home to over a thousand Irish, who constituted one-third of the city's total population. The large number of Catholics in Portland brought a visiting priest on an irregular basis beginning in 1830, and regular Catholic masses were held at a local home after 1837.

Middletown, anxious to lure laborers to town for its factories, encouraged Irish settlement. Henry DeKoven, in 1841, willed land for St. John's Roman Catholic Church, and the will was executed by Samuel Russell, owner of the city's largest manufacturing enterprise, Russell Manufacturing. The availability of the church increased the size of Middletown's Irish population, which eventually outgrew the 1842 church building. As plans were being made for a new church in 1850, it became apparent that the "welcome extended the Irish was more than verbal." (Hall) Middletown's Irish found they had friends in high places. Charles Richard Alsop, a wealthy resident involved in efforts to locate a railroad in Middletown, donated additional land, and Mrs. Richard (Aimee) Alsop, herself a Swiss Catholic, provided $500 toward the new church's construction. St. John's Church, completed in 1852, was built entirely of Portland brownstone, donated by the owners of the Portland quarries. In 1855, the old church was converted to a parochial school for Middletown's Catholic children, and Mr. Cody of County Cork, Ireland, was invited to be head of the school, assisted by two local sisters, Isabel and Helen Fagan. The school was reorganized by the Sisters of Mercy in 1873, who were housed in a convent built east of the church.

By 1850, the neighborhoods along the river, east of Main Street and surrounding St. John's Church, became home to most of the local Irish families. They lived in tenements which would later be occupied by immigrants from southern Europe. Irish women were hired as domestic servants, and laborers traveled by ferry to the Portland quarries. The second generation usually sought employment outside the quarries, at Middletown factories and stores. Those who had saved enough money to purchase property improved their economic situation by taking in boarders.

However, the Irish in Middletown, particularly those who came after 1850, were a transient group during the 1850s and 1860s. "Of the 792 Irish persons listed in the 1850 Middletown City Census, only 71, or 9 percent, were listed on the 1860 Census." (Milano) Some may have relocated to Portland to be closer to the quarries, but growing tension between labor and management at the quarries led many Irish to look for work elsewhere. By this time, Middletown factories increas-

Several members of the Chafee family, descendants of Irish immigrants, worked in saloons and restaurants on Main Street and on Court Street between 1870 and 1890. George A. Chafee opened the Chafee Hotel at 74 Court Street in 1893. The hotel offered a dining room, with banquet facilities used regularly by local fraternal groups, a tap room, and a barber shop. The building was partially razed in the 1950s and rebuilt by the Sons of Italy for a social hall.
Courtesy Sebastian "Mike" Marino

tricts, closer to their places of employment. By the turn of the century, Middletown had many Irish-American owned businesses, including James Donovan's Middlesex Plumbing and Heating store and McNulty and Murphy's Pharmacy. Middletown's chief of police, and most of his officers, were of Irish descent.

Until the arrival of immigrants from eastern and southern Europe, Irish-Americans comprised the largest non-English population in Middletown. The assimilation of the Irish-Americans accelerated with the arrival of the new immigrants, leaving the Irish as "old stock" in a town that now included Germans, Swedes, Jews, and Poles. Employers often hired those who could speak English and were familiar with the social order of northern European society. This acceptance hastened the dilution of the Irish-American community, and they increasingly married outside of their ethnic group. In 1900, 75 percent of Middletown's Irish-American population married other Irish-Americans. By 1920, the percentage had decreased to only 33, and it continued to decline until in 1950, a mere 5 percent of the descendants of Irish immigrants married within their ethnic group. (Coyle) □

ingly required skilled or semi-skilled labor and were not likely to hire unskilled, newly-arrived Irish immigrants.

Although there were several prosperous Irish-American residents in Middletown in the mid-nineteenth century, they were all descendants of those who had immigrated before 1820. Charles Brewer, a jeweler who owned five houses and four stores in 1850, and Jonathan Kilbourne, an innkeeper on South Main Street, probably came to Middletown with substantial capital. The Mortimers and the Magills, who descended from prosperous merchants and professional people of the late-eighteenth century, helped to elect Middletown's first Irish mayor in the 1850s, William Casey, whose father had immigrated in the 1790s. However, the Irish who came after 1820 did not improve their economic situation until the 1870s and 1880s. Of the seventy-one Irish-Americans who appeared on both the 1850 and 1860 Census, only six owned real estate.

During the 1870s, to boost the city's economy, banks in Middletown were eager to extend credit to allow Irish-Americans to buy homes and small businesses. More were able to find employment in factories, and several opened neighborhood stores. As immigrants from other European countries began arriving in the 1880s, Irish families left the tenements east of Main Street and built attractive homes in the North End and South Farms dis-

In 1906, this group of Irish men gathered for a parade on the west side of Main Street, just north of the Grand Street intersection. The Irish in Middletown participated in many community celebrations, including St. Patrick's Day which was celebrated in grand fashion, with a parade and an all-day party at the club owned by the Ancient Order of Hibernians on Spring Street. Irish-Americans came from Bridgeport and other cities in Connecticut for the celebration.
Courtesy Ann Grillo

When Lawton and Wall grocery store closed in 1905, Michael Wall and his son Timothy went into partnership with John T. Donovan, who had been a clerk at the store for many years. In 1911, after Michael Wall's death, Timothy moved to Cobalt and sold the store to John Donovan and his brother Joseph. They opened under the name of Donovan Brothers and were located on the east side of Main Street, just north of Ferry Street. The store provided delivery service throughout town, for which they stabled their horses on Green Street, where Joseph owned a home. With the success of the business, John was able to build three houses on Liberty Street. In this 1912 photograph, standing in the doorway of the store, are (left to right) John Donovan, Joseph Donovan, Hattie Donovan, and an unidentified man.
Courtesy Virginia Donovan

Hattie Donovan (right) was the daughter of John Donovan, co-owner of Donovan Brothers on Main Street. She was photographed, circa 1905, with her friend Julia Gray. Hattie lived on Liberty Street, near Park Place, and worked as a clerk at the James H. Bunce Company.
Courtesy Virginia Donovan

Flynn's Wine Room, circa 1905, was located on lower Court Street, just below Main. John Wiernasz (right), a Polish immigrant, served as the bartender for the establishment until he became a police officer in 1915.
Courtesy Anne Toczko Nowakoski

Sumner Street was photographed during a spring freshet, circa 1900, from the bridge over Sumner Brook. Until the 1930s, most of Middletown's Jewish residents lived in this neighborhood, along Sumner, Union, and South streets. Allison Brothers Soap Works, on the left, was located on Sumner Street from 1810 until it closed, about 1920. South Street intersects on the right.
Courtesy J. Russell "Doc" Ward

With a chupa *above their heads, Harry and Rose Shapiro are the first couple to be married in Middletown's synagogue on Union Street in 1911. Note that the altar, or* bima, *is located in the center, a plan that was characteristic of traditional Orthodox synagogues. Weddings were a community affair; the women would cook together, and according to custom, the bridal couple and all the guests would walk to the synagogue for the service. Courtesy Mrs. Max (Muriel Shapiro) Schulman*

The Jews

The first historical evidence of Jews in Middletown dates to the late eighteenth century when Isaac Solomons complained to the General Assembly about difficulties he experienced in importing goods from London. In 1776 Myer Myers, another Jewish resident of Middletown, invested in a local lead mine. Not until the 1870s, did Jews from Europe and Russia arrive in significant numbers. Many had experienced the loss of political rights, restrictions upon their business practices, and the denial of places to worship. America loomed as a land of opportunity and freedom.

Many of the earliest arrivals, in the late 1870s and early 1880s, from Austria-Hungary and Germany, were urban, prosperous, and influenced by the Reform Jewish movement that stressed the separation of spiritual and secular life. The larger group of Jewish immigrants that came from Poland, Russia, and eastern Europe between 1895 and 1920, emigrated from poorer rural regions where they had established a communal Yiddish culture that relied for its survival on Orthodoxy and spiritual tradition. Nevertheless, the established Jewish community embraced the newcomers, and eagerly joined the Jewish organizations established by the Orthodox group. A lively Jewish community developed along Sumner, Union, and South streets, with Jewish-owned bakeries, grocery stores, and butcher shops catering to the needs of the neighborhood.

Jewish immigrants provided labor for the large number of factories springing up in the area. The Eastern Tinware Company of Portland was a major employer of Jewish labor. From its main offices in Brooklyn, the Tinware Company recruited immigrants as they arrived in New York. When those offices closed in 1898, many Jews sought employment at the New England Enameling Company in Middletown, which opened in 1902. Middletown's thriving economy drew most of the Portland Jews to the opposite side of the river.

The incorporation of a synagogue was the next step for the group of Jews that concentrated in the South End of Middletown. The first *shul*, or synagogue, was in a Portland building that later housed the Keane Dance Studio. Harry Shapiro's Bar Mitzvah was held there in 1902. In Middletown, beginning in 1904, a room was rented over Max Frank's grocery store on William Street, and later, a larger space was leased on Main Street. The General Assembly approved the incorporation of the Congregation Adath Israel in 1905, and three years later the Jewish community purchased a two-family brick house on Union Street. The house was gutted to accommodate a Hebrew school on the ground floor and a synagogue on the second. The congregation was Orthodox and strictly adhered to the Jewish custom requiring women to sit in the balcony, apart from the men on the main floor. Adath Israel was able to build a larger and permanent synagogue in 1928 at the corner of Church and Broad streets. In 1942, the congregation joined the Conservative movement of the United Synagogue Council and abandoned separate seating for men and women. Relaxing their most orthodox practices, they also hired their first Conservative rabbi.

Before Hebrew classes were begun at the Union Street Synagogue, local Jewish boys were taught at home by melameds. Max Grower, father of Dr. Julius Grower, conducted the first Talmud

Israel Mittelman, a cobbler by trade, settled at the corner of Grand and Main streets in 1889, after immigrating from Austria-Hungary. When Mittelman applied for a business loan at a local bank, officers mistook his signature for "J. Mittelman" and filled out the paperwork accordingly. The error stuck and he opened J. Mittelman and Sons in 1910, a dry goods store often referred to in advertisements as "The Live Store." Mittelman, in the 1920s, was Middletown's first Jewish councilman.
Courtesy Irwin Mittelman

Singing in the Congregation Adath Israel choir was part of a boy's Hebrew education in 1913. Pictured here in the back row from left to right are: _____ Gordon, Isidore Mattes, _____ Mittleman, unidentified, and _____ Shapiro. The first row: Benny Levine, Isidore Rosenthal, Harry Frank, Rabbi Wiernikoff, _____ Baum, Maurice Shapiro, and Philip Markowitz.
Courtesy Mrs. Max (Muriel Shapiro) Schulman

For a short time J. A. Shapiro and Sons operated another store specializing in women's lingerie, located only a few doors down from their main store in the Mansion Block. Rose Shapiro, left, and Lillie Slutzky, a cousin, posed for this photo in 1921.
Courtesy Mrs. Max (Muriel Shapiro) Schulman

and Torah classes at the Union Street Synagogue. Even after classes were provided at the synagogue, girls were taught at home. The home and family were at the center of Jewish life. Parents instructed their children in the ritual of lighting candles for the Sabbath and the holidays, and in the way to wind the phylacteries, or boxes containing a declaration of their belief in God, around the forehead. Youth also learned the ceremonies necessary to observe the kosher dietary laws.

The congregation helped the entire community. A Ladies Aid Society, begun in 1903, provided social hours for Jewish inmates at the Connecticut State Hospital and rolled bandages for Middlesex Hospital. Money was raised to help poor farmers, and transient Jews were always offered a place to stay at the synagogue. Other Jewish community groups were organized, including the Adath Israel Sisterhood, Independent B'rith Abraham, and B'Nai B'rith lodges.

The growing community produced professional people such as William Citron, the first Jewish lawyer in Middletown, and Harry Frank and Julius Grower, the first physicians. Inspired by newfound prosperity, people began to leave the old neighborhood. Often the move was only to nearby William Street, but this was still considered a move up and out.

A 1979 study of marriage patterns among the ethnic groups in Middletown revealed that the Jewish population remained homogeneous longer than any other ethnic group in the community. (Coyle) In 1920, 1940, and 1960, 100 percent of local Jews married other Jews, but by 1979, the percentage had decreased to 33 percent. □

The Poles

The Poles were the first "new immigrants" to arrive in large numbers in Middletown after 1880. Persons of direct or mixed Polish ancestry make up the second largest ethnic group in Middletown. (1980 United States Census) Only Italian immigrants came in larger numbers. Between 1880 and 1920, Polish peasants emigrated to Middletown in search of economic opportunity, congregating in the area along lower College and William streets, known as "Duck Hollow" due to its frequent flooding. Their neighbors to the south were Jewish, many of whom also came from Poland, and a comfortable bond developed between the two groups.

Adapting to the industrial world was difficult for these Polish farmers. By 1880, enormous demand for unskilled labor in area factories provided Polish men with jobs at the Russell Manufacturing Company and Wilcox, Crittenden and Company. Yet most longed to return to the agrarian life they had known. Their chance came after 1900, when many Yankee farmers abandoned their family homesteads, unable to make agricultural production profitable. Polish families bought them out and rejuvenated farmsteads in Maromas and Westfield. Although most were not large commercial operations, the farms provided for family needs and supplemental income.

The first Pole in Middletown, John Rustaj, settled in Newfield in 1880. He was soon followed, in 1885, by Michael Niedziejko (Nejako), Francis Brzoznowski, and Thomas and Augustine Szhorkowski. By 1893, when the first Polish women arrived, there were forty-six men from Poland in Middletown.

These railroad tracks were at the foot of College Street. The houses on the right of this photograph faced Water Street. At the turn of the century, this area was known as "Duck Hollow" and was home to Middletown's Polish community.
Courtesy Colonel C. B. McCoid

Jacob Zawisza, in 1905, donned his full military regalia to participate with other St. Kazimierz Lancers in a parade to welcome Theodore Roosevelt to Middletown. With their silver buttons and colorful feathers, the Lancers were a wondrous sight.
Courtesy Violet (Ewanowski) Bladek

Carrying on the traditions of their homeland, Walter, Vincent, Steven, Elizabeth, and Joseph Zawisza participated in the first Easter procession after the completion of St. Mary's Church in 1905. Francis Nejako, at the time a student at Wesleyan University and later a Latin teacher at Middletown High School, organized the Easter festivities.
Courtesy Violet (Ewanowski) Bladek

It did not take long for the Polish community to produce successful businessmen, lawyers, policemen, and community leaders. John Wiernasz became the first Polish policeman in 1910, and Frances Nejako, the daughter of an early arrival, was the first Polish-American to graduate from Wesleyan (in 1907). A Latin teacher at Middletown High School for many years, she had Nejako Drive named in her honor. Alexander Guida married a local girl, Mary Majewski, in 1903 and eight years later bought a farm on Coleman Road. He built up the prosperous dairy farm that is still run by his sons as Sunshine Dairy.

In 1904, after years of attending Middletown's predominantly Irish St. John Church, or the Polish Catholic Church in New Britain, the Poles were granted permission to start their own parish. St. Mary of Czestochowa Church was completed on Hubbard Street in 1905. At that time there were over three hundred Polish families in Middltown. This first church was converted to St. Mary's School in 1911, when a larger church was needed. After an arsonist destroyed their beloved church on August 22, 1980, the Polish people immediately rebuilt St. Mary's on Hubbard Street.

Instrumental in the organization of St. Mary's Church was the St. Kazimierz Society of Polish Lancers, organized in 1902. A fraternal group, named for a fourteenth-century Polish king, the Lancers were dedicated to preserving the Polish religion and cultural inheritance. The society also helped newly arrived Poles adjust to life in Middletown. In 1940, the St. Kazimierz Society merged with the St. Joseph and Polish Knights societies to become the Polish National Home Corporation. The Polish Falcons, another fraternal society, was organized in 1913 and in 1931, bought Lakeview Park, a ten-acre park at Crystal Lake on Prout Hill Road, to provide a recreational area for Polish families. ☐

*Mary Bugaj Makuch, third from left,
posed with her bridesmaids, Zofie Bugaj
Kokoszka, Mary Kokoszka Zyjac, and*

*Honora Bugaj Basztura on her wedding
day in February 1910.
Courtesy Ann Moskal Salonia*

*Officer John Wiernasz wore Badge No. 1
in the late 1920s. Before becoming a
policeman in 1915, John Wiernasz was a
bartender at Flynn's Wine Room on Court
Street.*
Courtesy Anne Toczko Nowakowski

The bride and groom, Pawel Kurek and Katarzyna Kokoszka Kurek, seated third and fourth from the left, were married at St. Mary's Church in Middletown and gathered with the wedding party for this photograph, about 1910. The groom's brother, Michael Kurek, sits to the right of the bride and bridesmaid, Katarzyna Kokoszka (cousin of the bride), is standing at the far right.
Courtesy Ann Moskal Salonia

The Germans

Coming primarily from urban environments, German immigrants were well-prepared for the commercial and industrial society of late-nineteenth-century Middletown. The German community was made up of two groups—those with marketable skills for industrial employment, and those who had the capital to invest in small businesses. The Germans finding work in area factories tended to congregate in the South Farms district, along Front, Russell, and East Main streets, near their places of employment, primarily Wilcox, Crittenden and Company and Russell Manufacturing Company. Those Germans who had the financial means to start business enter-

prises—including Alexander Schmidt's laundry on Broad Street, Bielefield's Village Grocery adjacent to the Mansion Block and Jacob Steuck's Bakery at Main and Washington streets—achieved considerable respect in the community for the quality of their services.

In 1893, the German community established the German Evangelical Lutheran Church on High Street. The congregation was divided in 1901 over the issue of whether or not Lutherans could also be Masons. The factory workers, mostly fundamentalists, felt Masonic rituals contradicted their basic Christian beliefs, while the members of the German business community saw the Masons as merely a secular fraternal group. The working-

Gustav Loewenthal established this mill-work shop on Russell Street, near the present Flower Avenue, in 1896. Born in Germany in 1866, he arrived in Middletown at the age of eighteen and built one of Russell Manufacturing Company's mills, as well as several residences in the community. He later moved his millworks to Berlin Street, where the family continued the business until the 1970s.
From the 1898 Penny Press Illustrated Edition, *courtesy Mrs. Helen Raffuse*

class Germans organized St. John's Evangelical Lutheran Church, and built a church on East Main Street, closer to their neighborhood. (Today that church is Grace Evangelical Lutheran Church located on Randolph Road.) Any animosity that may have surfaced during the split, however, quickly dissipated.

In an effort to denationalize the perception of the German Evangelical Lutheran Church during World War I, the name was sandblasted from above the entrance and changed to St. Paul's Evangelical Lutheran Church. Many German-Americans from Middletown served in the United States Army, and only ten years later, Middletown elected its first mayor of German descent, Frederick Bielefield (mayor from 1926 to 1934). Bielefield's experience serves as an example of the assimilation of many of Middletown's German-Americans. Although he married a German woman, his family attended the Congregational church and joined the mainstream of community life. □

The Swedes
The Swedes were the smallest of Middletown's nineteenth-century immigrant groups. The Portland quarries were usually an early stop on the journey of immigrant Swedes, but because

they came from urban industrial backgrounds, they soon moved on to work in factories and the building trades. John Swenson, who arrived in 1870, was the first Swede in Middletown; he was followed in the 1880s by over a hundred Swedish families until immigration from Sweden virtually ended in 1900. The Swedes were drawn to America by the expanding American economy at a time when the Swedish economy was depressed. By 1900, when one-fifth of the world's Swedes resided in America, the opportunities in Sweden improved and emigration ended.

According to Dr. Sandberg of Hartford, "My folks, both of whom were born in Sweden, made no effort to teach Swedish . . . their kids were going to be Americans and were going to speak English. There was no feeling that we were going to hang onto our culture." (O'Connor and Sunderlind) Although the first generation congregated in a small Swedish neighborhood near Bridge Street and created a Swedish church and cultural organizations, by World War I, the second generation had abandoned their parents' way of life. The Swedish Evangelical Lutheran Tabor Church, built on High Street in 1895, loosened its ethnic ties to attract non-Swedes and went to English-only services in 1922. In 1958, the year a new church was built on Washington Street, the name was changed to Christ Evangelical Lutheran Church. Today, many parishioners are still of Swedish descent, and traditional celebrations, such as the Saint Lucia festival, have been revived. □

The Italians
According to the 1980 United States census, there are more people in Middletown of Italian, or mixed-Italian ancestry, than of any other ethnic group. Although several families came here from northern Italy in the latter part of the nineteenth century, it is the group from Melilli, Sicily, that has played a major role in creating the character of Middletown.

Angelo Magnano was the first Melillese in Middletown. His brother, Vincenzo, came to the United States in 1881 as the manager of a three-legged boy, a Sicilian hired by Barnum and Bailey's Circus in Bridgeport. Angelo visited Middletown in 1886 and returned permanently in 1895 with his family. He wrote home to two friends, Nicolo Saraceno and Luigi Annino, telling of the opportunities available for both tradesmen and unskilled workers.

The Melillesi were originally sojourners, coming to America to "make a fortune, and then return to Melilli, buy land, raise a family, and live like princes." (Sangree) Land was scarce in Sicily and opportunities limited. In America, employ-

The Vorwaerts (meaning "Forward") Society was formed in 1907 as a social organization for working-class Germans. In this photograph, circa 1910, the founders and their families posed on the lawn of their South Front Street hall during a picnic. Often referred to as the "Dutch" or "Deutsch" Club, the group held social affairs featuring German singing groups from around Connecticut and beer brewed on the premises.
Courtesy Club Vorwaerts

ment and housing were available. A Melillese neighborhood on the east side of town provided support and a sense of belonging. Some families returned to Melilli, but most made Middletown their home.

The streets leading to the river from Main Street, which had once been home to most of Middletown's Irish population, became predominantly occupied by Italian immigrants. In the area near the riverfront, along Rapallo Avenue, Green Street, Ferry Street, and Court Street, during the 1920s, one could dine on "the best Italian Spaghetti" at D'Amico Tavern, buy "Special Tomato Pies" at Marino's Bakery, shop on Ferry Street at Amenta's Grocery and Corvo's Grocery, or order fresh meat at Messini's Butcher Shop. It was a self-sufficient community, where families grew their vegetables in their front-lawn gardens, spoke Italian to their neighbors and children, and preserved the old ways of Melilli.

Most immigrants found jobs in area factories as unskilled workers until they learned English

and sought better employment. Others marketed their skills as construction workers, carpenters, and masons. In 1904, Vincenzo and Angelo Magnano saved enough to buy a large tenement at the foot of Center Street, called the "Lighthouse" because it stood out from a distance as one came down the river. It became home to many Italian families, who nicknamed it *La Batteria*, or "madhouse," a humorous reference to the constant activity that went on at the house. Professional men came out of Middletown's Italian community, like Louis LaBella and Joseph Magnano, who were physicians, and Vincent Scamporini and Joseph Adorno, attorneys. The Saraceno brothers built Capitol Theater on Main Street. But many Italians worked endless hours at places like Russell Manufacturing, Palmer Mills, or Noiseless Typewriter Company, and were unable to prosper.

Maintaining Melillese tradition became harder as the children of the original immigrants were influenced by American society. They were edu-

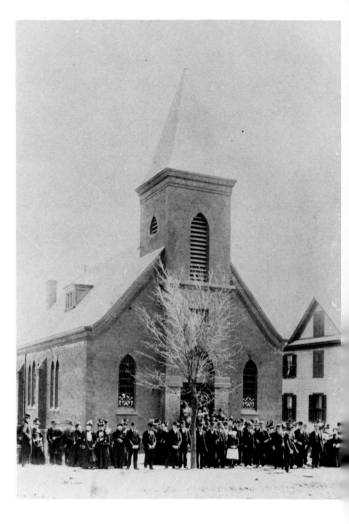

St. Paul's Evangelical Lutheran Church on High Street, about 1910. Fire gutted the church on the day before Christmas in 1955, requiring the congregation to rebuild.
Courtesy Oscar G. Lenz Family

Carl Herrmann opened a liquor store and delicatessen on Main Street about 1910. The store was a Middletown landmark for over sixty years, respected for its home-made baked goods and wide selection of imported products. Joseph Rajtar and Joe Cyrulik, store employees, hold the largest bologna ever imported to Middletown, about 1930.
Courtesy Carl F. Herrmann

cated in public schools and learned English. They had contact with children of other backgrounds, like the Polish children in the neighborhood to the south. Traditionally, marriages were arranged through the parents. When a young man considered asking a woman to marry him, his parents approached her family about the matter, and the adults would have final approval. When Josie Lombardo decided that she wanted to marry Lewis Gage of Higganum in 1940, she knew she could not expect his parents to ask for her hand. Fortunately, after only minor objections, Josie's parents agreed to the marriage, aware that customs were changing in their small community. (Lombardo) Yet, in 1940, more than half of all Italian-Americans in Middletown married within their ethnic group. But by 1960, only 26.6 percent of Middletown's residents of Italian descent married other Italian-Americans. (Carrington Coyle,

1980) The Italian-American men and women who fought in World War II served with people of different backgrounds, and returned with broadened expectations for the future. By 1955, Italian-Americans owned half of all the city's grocery stores, and one-third of the gas stations. (Lombardo) However, with the help of Italian fraternal organizations such as the Sons of Italy and the Garibaldi Society, as well as the church, subsequent generations have maintained their Italian identity, and perpetuated Melillese traditions. □

Other Immigrants

Immigrants from China, Scotland, England, Portugal, Denmark, and Greece also sought opportunity in Middletown, albeit in smaller numbers, and have contributed to the character of the community. □

Alice and Lillian Bauer, seen here in 1915, were the daughters of Conrad Bauer, a weaver, who came from Germany about 1884 and built a house on Front Street.
Courtesy Barbara Molander Warner, permission Lillian (Bauer) Crowell

CARL HERRMANN

FOR STATE
REPRESENTATIVE

– Pull Top Lever –

Carl Herrmann, Jr., went to work for his father in 1917 and operated the store until it closed in 1974. He oversaw the creation of a private label of liquor imported from Scotland, called "Racer's Pride" in honor of his love of horse racing. He ran, unsuccessfully, for state representative in 1948.
Courtesy Carl F. Herrmann, Jr.

Owing to an economic depression, congregants built the Lutheran church themselves. Each male member was required to donate two days labor or pay $1.50 per day, at a time when most workers made only 75 cents a day. The church members taking a break from construction are: (back row) John Fox, Edward Lundberg, Charles Bengtson, unidentified, Emil Ehlberg, unidentified, Godfrey Carlson, Axel Lundberg, unidentified, unidentified, Henry Hanson, and Perry Closson; (second row) Burton Carlson, Gustav Johnson, and Ernest Adamson; (front row) Andrew Carlson, Emil Olson, Fred Anderson, Arthur Carlson, and Carl Carlson.
Courtesy Christ Evangelical Lutheran Church

The Swedish Evangelical Lutheran Church on High Street, is seen here about 1900. Later occupied by the Shiloh Baptist Church, the building was destroyed by fire in 1973.
Courtesy Everett Wright

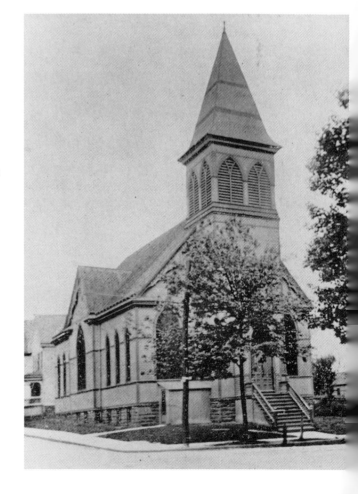

Tena Johnson, right, was a milliner on Bridge Street in the late nineteenth century. The Bridge and Miller street neighborhood was home to many Swedish families during this period. In 1900, after she married John Anderson, another Swedish immigrant, she moved her business to Rapallo Avenue.
Courtesy John Irving Anderson Family

Robert E. Molander (left front) posed with Oscar Englum (right rear) and two other Swedish friends from their Bridge Street neighborhood about 1915. Robert Molander married Frances Mann, a local woman of Scottish descent, just before he left for service in World War I.
Courtesy Barbara Molander Warner

Robert, Nanette, Olga, and Esther Molander pose with their mother, Clara, in 1903, the year their father, Anton, died. Anton and Clara Molander came to Middletown from Sweden in 1887. The family lived and ran a saloon at 95 Bridge Street. Robert E. Molander began working at the James H. Bunce Company at the age of fourteen and was named its president upon the death of James Bunce in the 1930s.
Courtesy Barbara Molander Warner

Felice Micone's grocery store opened for business on Bridge Street in 1899. He also operated a saloon nearby after 1905. Courtesy J. Russell "Doc" Ward

The "Festa di San Sebastiano," as a traditional Melillese festival, dates back to 1414 when a shipwreck on the Sicilian coast washed ashore a chest containing a statue of Saint Sebastian. Taken as a sign of God's favor, the statue was worshipped as the patron saint of Melilli and laden with jewelry. The original church of St. Sebastian was built on the site where the statue came to rest when it washed ashore. The Feast of Saint Sebastian began in Middletown in 1908, when Sebastian Marchese (shown here, circa 1932) sculpted a replica of Melilli's statue and displayed it on his front porch on Ferry Street. The neighbors paid homage to the saint by bringing food and wine. In the years from 1909 to 1911, Ferry Street neighbors would chip in to string electric lights over the street, and an Italian band, led by "Nino" Amenta, provided music for dancing. Money was pinned to the statue as it was carried aloft through the streets of the Italian neighborhood. In 1913, the statue was moved from Marchese's front porch to Santo Cannata's store on Court Street, and the Court Street playground next to the railroad tracks became the site of the festivities. With money collected during the feast, the Italian-American community built a church in honor of and named for St. Sebastian. Since the completion of the church in 1931, the feast has been held there every year during the third weekend in May. Courtesy Max Corvo Collection

Antonio "Nino" Amenta, seen here in 1906, was a well-educated man. Amenta worked for Guy and Rice, a travel and insurance agency, arranging passage for Melillese laborers needed at local factories. It was through this type of network that so many Melillese came to this city. The Amentas also owned a grocery store on Ferry Street. Courtesy Italio "Pat" Amenta

Dr. Louis LaBella volunteered his time to teach neighborhood kids baseball at Wadsworth Playground, where the Superior Court now stands on DeKoven Drive. From left to right are Sal Lombardo, Joe Cannata, Mike Cannata, Johnny Garafolo, Pat Tomassi, Salvatore Salafia, Whitey Cannata (between knees), Phil Salafia,

Hickey Cannata, Joe Amato, and Carl Lombardo in 1924. Sports clubs were organized between 1910 and 1940 and included the Get-There Football Team, the Liberty Athletic Club Basketball Team, and the Speed Boys Basketball Team. *Courtesy Phil Salafia*

World featherweight boxing champion, Willie Pep, was born William Gugliermo Papaleo in Middletown in 1922. His first prize-winning fight was in Madison Square Garden in 1942, followed by sixty-two consecutive wins. Although his career was interrupted by severe injuries received in a 1947 plane crash, he continued to fight until 1966. Willie Pep, who now resides in Wethersfield, recently retired as athletic inspector for the state of Connecticut. *Courtesy Max Corvo Collection*

Initially, the Italians attended St. John's Roman Catholic church on Main Street. With funds from the "Festa" and money donated by the Italian community, a replica of Melilli's Church of St. Sebastian was built in 1931. Local Italian carpenters, stone masons, bricklayers and laborers donated their time to its construction. The church (shown here, circa 1940) is of Italian Renaissance design, and built of grey Weymouth granite, topped by a tile roof. The interior features Carrara marble in the sanctuary, used for the altar, flooring, pulpit, and railing. The murals on the ceiling, depicting the Apostles and St. Sebastian, emphasize the height and grandeur of the church. *Courtesy Max Corvo Collection*

Marino's Bakery truck, driven by Tony Marino, was stopped on Ferry Street in 1938. Once part of a thriving Italian neighborhood, the bakery was located near several other businesses owned by Sicilian immigrants, including Amenta's grocery store, Corvo's store, and the DiGiandomenico greenhouses. Marino's Restaurant and Bakery is one of the few Italian-American businesses still operating on Ferry Street, most having closed or relocated when subsequent generations of Melillese left the North End.
Courtesy Tillie Milardo

In 1933 Alfio Colonghi posed between two Navy buddies for this photograph in Mexico, during the time he was stationed in San Diego, California, aboard the U.S.S. Trenton. The character of the ethnic communities in Middletown changed after World War II. The sons and daughters of the Melillese immigrants returned from war envisioning greater opportunity. Many veterans who would otherwise have been unable to attend college took advantage of the G.I. bill to further their education, get better jobs, and move out of the old neighborhoods.
Photograph courtesy Jennie DiGiandomenico

Tony Pastor (1907-1969), nationally known musician and bandleader of the thirties and forties, was a Middletown native son. Born Tony Pestritto to Melillese parents, he went on to play with the Artie Shaw Band and other famous big band orchestras. In the North End, where Pastor grew up, several boys played instruments and were fascinated by jazz. Tony's father bought him a saxophone and arranged for lessons with Lucio Pandolfini, a local Melillesian graduate of the Conservatory of Music in Palermo, Italy. After making rapid progress on the saxophone, Tony played with the Luistro-Annino Orchestra, a Middletown band that played area clubs and the Moodus summer resorts. By 1925, Tony was a well-respected musician in the Middletown area, and eventually he was noticed by nationally-known bands. During the thirties he became famous for his solo on "Begin the Beguine" with the Artie Shaw Band, and he also accompanied singers like Rosemary Clooney. Shown here is the cover of a 1961 album Tony Pastor (left) made with his children in Las Vegas. Courtesy Rose Pestritto Tommasi

James Findley Mann, pictured here with his son Hamilton, was a Scottish laborer living in England before coming to America in 1880. A brass finisher by trade, he came to Middletown in 1890 where he was employed by the trolley company making brass fixtures and hardware. Courtesy Barbara Molander Warner

121

FRUIT SPECIALTIES
"LESVOS"
CIGARS & TOBACCO

GREEK
PRODUCE

CANADA DRY

Costas "Gus" Xenelis, right, shown here in 1928 with employee Stanley Grabek, opened the Lesvos Fruit Store, with his father, Nicholas Xenelis, in 1923. The store, located on the west side of Main Street, just south of College Street, was named for the Greek island where Costas and Nicholas Xenelis had been born. At the time Xenelis opened his fruit store, the Greek-American Company, owned by James Bravakis, sold fruit and ice cream near the corner of Main and William streets. The northern half of Xenelis' building had served as the first police station, from 1882 to 1887. Gus Xenelis is still operating his store, today known as Middlesex Fruitery, with the help of his son, Ted, and daughter-in-law, Mary, in the same location.
Courtesy Xenelis Family

Ludwig and Astrid Hoffman came from Denmark with their three boys, Gunnar, Carl, and Robert, in 1907. Astrid's sister and brother-in-law, Martha and George Eriksson, immigrated with their three children in 1913, when this photograph was taken. Ludwig worked for the telephone company beginning in 1910. Astrid and Ludwig are in the center of the photograph, she with her arm around her husband. Martha Eriksson lounges in front with her children, in white, nearby. Courtesy Doris Lee

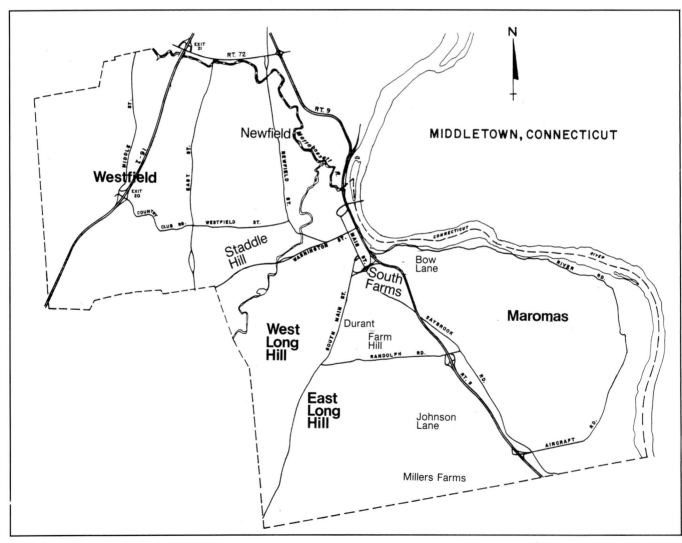

Westfield was almost exclusively a farming community until the J. O. Smith Manufacturing Company began operations in 1826. John Smith, an English emigre, bought Nathaniel Bacon's rum distillery and commenced the manufacture of Japan finishes, a type of paint that required baking to provide a smooth, lustrous finish. After fire destroyed the original mill in 1874, his son, James Owen Smith, built the factories shown here, and enlarged the company's product line to include varnishes, enamels, and tinware, such as cash boxes and typewriter covers. Today these factory buildings are occupied by Raymond Engineering. Photograph, circa 1880, courtesy Colonel C. B. McCoid

The Outlying Neighborhoods

Rural enclaves were established throughout Middletown as the sons and grandsons of the first settlers occupied the extensive outlying lands allocated to their families in the seventeenth century. Several of the larger villages, such as Upper Houses (Cromwell), East Middletown (Portland), Chatham (East Hampton), and Middlefield, eventually became incorporated as separate towns. The rural outlying areas that remained a part of Middletown were referred to by names that described their locations: the west field, the south farms, the new field, and the long hill. Each of these enclaves was dominated by subsequent generations of the early settler families, and by the nineteenth century the neighborhoods established self-contained societies that allowed them to function somewhat independently from the rest of Middletown. Westfield, Maromas, Long Hill, Newfield, Staddle Hill, and South Farms established district schools, social halls, and, in two instances, churches, that helped them shape distinct personalities. When the central part of Middletown was incorporated as a city in 1784, the outlying neighborhoods were designated as the "Town of Middletown." During the 1870s, the larger regions in the town splintered into fourteen school districts that were governed by the city, but taxed separately and required to finance their own schools. This awkward separation between governance and taxation existed until 1959. Many of the names given to the school districts have survived as tax, school, and fire districts, or as street names. ☐

Westfield

The Wilcox, Bacon, Atkins, and Higby families were among the first settlers of Westfield in the 1720s and 1730s. This northwestern part of town, at the time bordered by the villages of Middlefield, Cromwell, and Newfield, as well as the town of Meriden, was a farming community. Although Westfield was comparable in area to Middlefield, the population was never as large as Middlefield's: in 1815 there were 93 families and 81 houses in Westfield; in 1852, 120 families occupied 104 dwellings.

Westfield's heydey as a farming community began when the port at Middletown boomed in the 1750s, and the farmers of Westfield shifted from growing crops to grazing cattle, horses, sheep, and pigs for the West Indian trade. During the American Revolution beef and grain were required for the Continental Army. The end of the Revolution in 1787, and the decline of trade after 1807, marked the end of Westfield's agricultural prosperity.

Farmers in most of Connecticut competed against increased production from richer land to the west. Industries took over land that had been used for farming, and drew labor to work in the mills. After 1790, the sons of Westfield farmers sought opportunity in the Western Reserve or took up new trades in the city. Farms were abandoned, or bought out by newcomers. Those that stayed in Westfield were unable to make their farms profitable owing to years of using poor farming techniques. Learned men, such as Reverend Jared Eliot of Killingworth, preached the use of radically innovative soil conservation techniques as early as 1748. Eliot recommended worn-out farmland be planted with clover for several seasons, to allow the soil's nutrients to be restored. He encouraged the drainage of wet lands, the use of manure for fertilization, and the development of a staple crop by Connecticut farmers. However, these suggestions were ignored, except by the most progressive farmers. Therefore, by 1840, commercial farming became unprofitable; production between 1800 and 1840 dropped 69 percent, statewide. (*Middletown Press* Centennial Edition, 1984)

Haddam and Middlefield experienced similar

The Methodists built this church in 1881 adjacent to the Miner Street Cemetery, near the intersection of Smith Street. The church membership was never large enough to support a minister, therefore the church relied on divinity students from Wesleyan University to conduct services. The existence of a Methodist Church caused conflict in this community of stalwart Congregationalists. Two sisters, Cordelia and Emily Graves, divided their Middle Street home, one side for the Congregationalist sister and one side for the Methodist sister. After the passing of this generation about 1920, membership in the Methodist Church declined and the church was converted to a dwelling. Courtesy Colonel C. B. McCoid

Horace Wilcox, whose family had resided on Atkins Street since the early eighteenth century, came from a long line of silverware makers and peddlers. In the 1870s, he expanded his family's enterprises and moved to Meriden to establish the Silver Manufacturing Company, the forerunner to International Silver Corporation (Insilco Corporation). Although he remained active in the Westfield community, his entrepreneurial legacy became part of Meriden's history.

Four district schools were located in Westfield during the nineteenth century, until the consolidated school was opened in 1910 for children throughout the district. Although Middletown High School was available after 1849 for older youths, the trek from Westfield to Middletown's center was long and difficult. Students from the outlying areas of Middletown were also required to take an entrance exam to be admitted to Middletown High, because the town of Middletown had less rigorous educational standards than the city district. In the late nineteenth century, trolley lines made downtown schools accessible and a majority of Westfield's young people took advantage of the

declines in agricultural production, but rebounded through the development of industry. Westfield never experienced industrial growth on the same scale. John Smith's manufacturing enterprise for the production of Japan paint, begun in 1826, was the only industry of consequence in the district. Japan paint was a type of lacquer, impervious to moisture and heat, that had to be baked at high temperatures. His enterprise also made containers for shipping the paint and later expanded to make stationery supplies that were coated with Japan paint for sale in moist regions, such as the Netherlands and Southeast Asia. Irish immigrants moved to Westfield as labor for the factory. During the latter part of the nineteenth century, as agriculture continued to decline, the Irish bought farms abandoned by older Yankee families. Near the turn of the twentieth century, the MacDonnell's Clay Pits and Brick Yard opened at Smith and Middle streets (present site of Olin Ski Company) and hired first-generation Italians, together with black laborers, for its seasonal operation. These laborers did not experience the welcome extended the Irish earlier in the century, and most chose to reside in West Cromwell and East Berlin.

The neighborhood near Miner and East streets was the center of community life in Westfield. Located there was the Greek Revival-style Third Congregational Church (right) and the church's lecture hall and Sunday school (left). The church was constructed in 1849 and still remains a vital part of the Westfield community. The Sunday school shown here had been a residence until 1865 when the church converted it for their use. It has since been connected to the church by an ell housing educational facilities. The neighborhood was also the site of one of the four district schools and the Westfield Grange. At one time the Grange membership was large enough to sponsor its own agricultural fair. Courtesy Colonel C. B. McCoid

Horace Wilcox, founder and owner of the silversmith enterprise in Meriden, built the Highland Country Club in Westfield in the mid-1880s. Catering to the wealthy of Middletown and Meriden, the club had its own trolley line, golf course, and pond, located on the hill north of Country Club Road. When the clubhouse, shown here, burned about 1918, a new structure was built. Membership dropped off after World War II. The club eventually closed and the building was left abandoned. Courtesy Colonel C. B. McCoid

opportunity. After the trolleys were discontinued in the 1930s, students were required to find their own way to the school. Not until after World War II and the advent of improved bus service could Westfield residents again avail themselves of the education available to the broader community.

By the 1960s, Westfield had become predominately a community of commuters working in Hartford, Meriden, and downtown Middletown. The construction of Route 91 divided the Westfield district in half. With the decision of the city to establish the I-91 industrial corridor and with the opening of I-91's Exit 20 off Country Club Road in 1971, as well as the subsequent extension of area sewers, Westfield became prime acreage for industrial development. More than four hundred acres of farmland in Westfield, owned primarily by the MacInerney family, was targeted in 1973 for the Sawmill Race Track. Ronald Mooney, a Canadian businessman, was able to obtain state and local permits to build what was to be the only horse track in the state of Connecticut. Plans for the track proceeded in 1974 after a city referendum approved its construction, and the Connecticut Court of Appeals rejected a petition submitted by Middletown's Citizen's Against the Race Track (C.A.R.T.) to ban the track. By 1980, plans for the Sawmill Race Track had been abandoned when Mooney was unable to arrange financial backing. Aetna Life & Casualty's Employee Benefits Division was built in 1983 on part of the land set aside for the race track, and remaining parcels were made available for industrial use. The people of Westfield, who have fought against random development, organized an association, Westfield Residents for Rational Development of Middletown, in 1980. But increasingly, Westfield's pastures and farmlands have given

way to condominiums and housing developments. □

Long Hill

The Long Hill neighborhood, taking its name from a succession of hills that extend southward to the Durham line, consists of a vast area, 3 miles long and 1.75 miles across, in the southern and southeastern part of Middletown. It is bounded by Randolph Road, the Durham border, the Middlefield line, and the South Farms district. Long Hill, unlike Westfield and Maromas, is still occupied by many descendants of the original seventeenth- and eighteenth-century settlers, such as the Hubbard, Wilcox, Roberts, Kelsey, Atkins, and Daniels families. As in other rural districts of Middletown, the families of Long Hill established a homogeneous community through intermarriage. Although Long Hill comprised a large corner of the town, the farms were scattered owing to Long Hill's hilly and rocky terrain. The population was never large enough to warrant a separate church parish.

With the establishment of two school districts in Long Hill in the 1870s, the region was divided into West Long Hill and East Long Hill. East Long Hill was designated as the area abutting the South Farms District, between the eastern end of Randolph Road and the town of Durham, and was separated from West Long Hill by the Durham Road (South Main Street). Although, to modern residents, East Long Hill seems close to the center of town, in the seventeenth century this back district was considered a remote community. In 1675, three stone blockhouses were constructed in Long Hill for defense against Indian attack. When the threat subsided, one of the remaining blockhouses in East Long Hill was converted to a schoolhouse.

It has since been adapted for use as a residence and still stands on Maple Shade Road, just east of Randolph Road. In 1878, Thomas Atkins, who wrote a history of Middlefield and Long Hill, counted thirty-seven houses in East Long Hill. Along Arbutus Street, Kelsey Street, Randolph Road, and Maple Shade Road, the homes were occupied by families who grew staple crops such as rye and corn, and raised livestock. Many of the early farms developed into commercial dairy farms, including the Crowell property on Coleman Road, which was owned by William A. Coleman, a successful dairy farmer, until the late 1930s.

The social life of the district revolved around two public buildings that stood on the Durham Road (Route 17) near the intersection of Randolph Road: Long Hill Union Chapel and the Lyceum.

Madeline and Marjorie Smith posed in 1905 wearing their new winter hats. Great-grandchildren of the founder of J. O. Smith Manufacturing Company, these girls lived on the street that bears his name.
Courtesy Colonel C. B. McCoid

Westfield Falls, near the foot of Higby Mountain on the Falls Brook, was a popular place in the nineteenth century for picnics and family photographs. The waterfall was used as a postcard scene well into the twentieth century. Today the falls can be seen from Route 91 but are accessible only by a dirt path from Miner Street.
Photograph, circa 1890, courtesy Colonel C. B. McCoid

Both were built in the late 1870s. The chapel provided non-denominational religious services, and the Lyceum was used for community dances and other social activities. In 1918, the Lyceum was razed for construction of the new Long Hill School, to provide West and East Long Hill with a modern, unified educational facility. The school served as a town elementary school until the late 1960s and was demolished in 1988 in anticipation of the construction of a housing development in the open land between Brown Street, Route 17, and Randolph Road.

From the mid-nineteenth century until World War II, East Long Hill experienced little growth or change. Frank Roberts, whose nineteenth-century ancestors built most of the early houses in the immediate area, took over his father's dairy business on Maple Shade Road in 1928 and operated a commercial vegetable farm until a few years ago. Under the impact of the housing boom following World War II, he has seen the character of East Long Hill change from self-contained farming village to suburban residential neighborhood. New streets were laid out through the pastures and fields of ancestral farms, and single- and multi-family housing units now fill the landscape.

West Long Hill was established in the region west of the Durham Road (Route 17) and south to the Middlefield border. Atkins counted 46 houses in West Long Hill in 1878. On Randolph Road, just west of the intersection of Route 17, the house built by Robert Hubbard in 1719 integrates another of the remaining stone blockhouses built for defense against Indians in 1675. The first floor of the house is built of brownstone rubble and is identical to the other blockhouse on Maple Shade Road, less than a quarter of a mile to the east. Hubbard added a wood-frame second floor which provided the structure with its typical colonial appearance. Later members of the Hubbard family farmed the land near the present intersection of Long Hill and Randolph roads, a farm that remains in operation today. The extensive lands further south were farmed by members of the Daniels family. Their early-nineteenth-century farmhouse is presently occupied by The Little People's School, and their barns are part of the Wesleyan Hills housing development. The Daniels's farmland was purchased in 1968 by the Hill Development Corporation, affiliated with Wesleyan University, and became the site of Middletown's first planned residential development. The first single-family houses were completed on the hill south of Long Hill Road by 1971, and the open land surrounding it was left untouched to provide a rural context. Since 1975, the Wesleyan Hills development has significantly expanded to include 270 condominium units and over 250 single-family homes, and some 200 additional units are currently being planned.

Closer to the district's western border, along Laurel Brook Road and Wadsworth Street, the Hubbard, Barnes, and Atkins families developed family and community ties with the people of Rockfall, a village in Middlefield adjacent to West Long Hill. One of the oldest houses remaining in this area is the Nehemiah Hubbard House, built in 1744, at the intersection of Laurel Brook Road and Wadsworth Street. Hubbard was a prominent banker and merchant in Middletown, yet he still carried on extensive farming on the property near his home. He served as deputy quartermaster during the Revolution and became the first president of the Middletown National Bank. His son, Nehemiah Hubbard, Jr., built a large Greek Revival house on Main Street, which later provided the columns for Colonel Wadsworth's estate in West Long Hill. Many of the houses that stood on Laurel Brook Road in the eighteenth and nine-

The Middletown Branch Line to Berlin, opened in 1850, had a depot near the foot of East Street, serving Westfield and West Cromwell. By the time this photograph was taken in 1940, the tracks were leased to the New York, New Haven and Hartford Railroad. The Little River Post Office is partially visible to the left of the depot. Both structures have since been torn down. In 1882, a line from Meriden to Cromwell intersected with the main line, a direct result of the efforts of Horace C. Wilcox, the owner of the Silver Manufacturing Company in Meriden, who wanted river access for transporting his silver products, thus circumventing the New York to Hartford railroad line to save expenses. Courtesy Colonel C. B. McCoid

teenth centuries have disappeared, their sites reclaimed by forest.

When Clarence Wadsworth married his cousin, Katherine Fearing Hubbard, they both brought wealth and large landholdings to the marriage. Wadsworth, raised in New York, inherited the DeKoven House on Washington Street from his mother Cornelia DeKoven Wadsworth. But it was his wife's land in Long Hill that was most valuable to him. Katherine Hubbard Wadsworth's ancestors had resided in Long Hill for two centuries and had accumulated extensive acreage along Laurel Brook and Little Falls, as well as in Middlefield. In 1909, the two retreated to Long Hill and built a mansion designed in the style of Academic Classicism. Wadsworth's true passion was forestry and park development, and he and his wife set out to create a park on their 250-acre estate. They laid paths through the woods and constructed fieldstone arch bridges over the streams. Wadsworth founded the Rockfall Corporation in 1935 "to establish, maintain and care for parks and forest or wild land for the use and enjoyment of the public." After his death in 1941, Wadsworth's park was turned over to the Connecticut State Park and Forest Commission and opened as a state park facility. Wadsworth

left the DeKoven House to the Rockfall Corporation, which opened the building to the public as a community center, providing offices for charitable and non-profit organizations.

South Farms

The South Farms district covers a large area bordered by Maromas to the north and west, Long Hill on the south, and the City district on the east. During the eighteenth and early nineteenth centuries the farms were scattered, and clusters of families established smaller neighborhoods within South Farms. In the 1870s, these smaller neighborhoods were organized into five school districts. After this time, the term *South Farms* became associated with the southernmost section of the region, the commercial and residential neighborhood along what is today East Main Street. The other school districts of South Farms—Bow Lane, Johnson Lane, Millers Farms, Farm Hill, and Durant—each developed differently during the nineteenth and twentieth centuries.

South Farms Neighborhood

South Farms, as a specific neighborhood, had by the 1840s become identified with the commercial center established near the junction of East Main Street and the Middlesex Turnpike (presently Saybrook Road). The success of Russell Manufacturing Company and Sanseer Mill on East Main Street spawned grocery stores, churches, and multi-family houses along East Main, Baer, and Elm streets. In 1869, Christ Church, later the Church of the Holy Trinity, constructed a Carpenter-Gothic-style branch church at the crossroads to cater to the growing population in South Farms. Later in the century, high-style homes were built by managers and superintendents of the manufacturing companies. Silver Street became one of Middletown's most exclusive residential neighbor-

hoods during the 1880s and 1890s, particularly for downtown retail businessmen and manufacturers.

Bow Lane

A corner of the Bow Lane district was chosen as the site for the Connecticut Hospital for the Insane in 1869, and the part of the district near the Middlesex Turnpike (Bow Lane and Saybrook Road) was affected by the development in South Farms associated with the growth of Russell Manufacturing Company. However, families in the southeastern section of the Bow Lane district, beyond the state hospital, maintained their agrarian way of life well into the twentieth century. The Tryon family farmed a considerable amount of land, and two houses associated with the family still stand on Bow Lane.

Johnson Lane and Millers Farms

Johnson Lane and Millers Farms were rural farming districts until after World War II. Millers Farms was located near the base of the Durham foothills, north of the present Millers Pond. The families in Millers Farms developed kinships with either Durham families or their nearest neighbors in the Johnson Lane district. Virtually unaffected by industrial or commercial growth occurring in Middletown, the families in Johnson Lane established a strong social network within their own neighborhood. Farmhouses were scattered along the roadways today known as Millbrook Road, Lee Street, Prout Hill Road, and Lyceum Road, and were occupied by many of the families that remain in the district today. Warren and Elvira Lee, who raise Hereford cattle for breeding stock, manage the farm begun by his grandfather, Daniel Lee, over one hundred years ago. The Harris family has lived in the district since the early nineteenth century and still operates a working farm on Wilcox Road. Many members of the Hubbard,

Photographed in 1930, this view of the Hezekiah Sage house, built in 1770, was taken from a hill looking east toward Atkins Street (formerly West Street). This type of rural scene was typical in Westfield until the mid-twentieth century. Easy access to Route 91, by way of Exit 20, has fostered industrial and corporate growth since the 1970s. The availability of large tracts of open land has led to random development of condominiums and housing developments.
Courtesy Colonel C. B. McCoid

Silas W. Roberts stands outside his house on Maple Shade Road, circa 1890, with his wife and children. The house remains at the intersection of Maple Shade and Randolph roads. The Roberts family was among the earliest residents of East Long Hill, and many descendants still live in the community.
Courtesy Kate Roberts Place

A group of friends from East Long Hill gathered in 1893 for this photograph. Front row, left to right, are Rachel (Sedrick) Wilcox, Mr. Lord, and Mrs. Frank Hubbard. Second row: unidentified, Mrs. Robert Hubbard, Mrs. Giles Taylor, unidentified, and unidentified. Third row: Mr. Ashton, unidentified, Mr. Robert Hubbard, Mrs. Ashton, and unidentified. Fourth row: Ida Roberts, Mrs. Holmes, Mrs. David Crowell, unidentified, and Edwin J. Roberts.
Courtesy Frank and Mildred Roberts

131

Daniels, and Roberts families also live in the Johnson Lane district. In the late nineteenth century, the neighborhood was tied together by the district school that stood on Millbrook Road, just south of Lyceum Road. The Lyceum was a social hall where the community held parties, sing-alongs, and weddings. The lyceum building still stands on Millbrook Road, at the head of Lyceum Road. It has been converted to a residence. In the late 1920s, several young men of the district organized "the Beeler Boys," a social group that sponsored neighborhood picnics, baseball games, and other activities. The group has remained active through the efforts of the present Johnson Lane families.

Farm Hill and Durant

The Farm Hill district runs north to south along Ridge Road and Hunting Hill Avenue, and abuts the Durant district, which runs parallel with South Main Street from Hunting Hill Avenue to Highland Avenue. Before Russell Manufacturing and, later, Wilcox, Crittenden and Company, made their mark on these neighborhoods, they were sparsely populated by farming families. The northern end of the Farm Hill district, near Prout Hill Road, still retains its rural character. With the growth of industry in the 1860s and 1870s, Farm

Hill developed as a residential neighborhood. The first houses were constructed on Ridge Road by prosperous downtown businessmen and the managers from the factories. After immigrants arrived in large numbers, the streets near Russell Manufacturing, including Front Street, South Front Street, and Fowler Avenue, became home to many of the factories' skilled and unskilled workers. The employees of the industries along the Pamaecha River—including Rogers and Hubbard Company and Wilcox, Crittenden and Company—established residential neighborhoods along Durant Street, Lake Avenue, and Russell Street in the late nineteenth century. The laying of trolley lines and the continued prosperity of the industries in South Farms encouraged suburban growth after the turn of the century. The concentration of working-class families in this neighborhood led the Consolidated School District of the Town of Middletown to choose the site at the northwest corner of Hunting Hill Avenue and Russell Street for a new high school in 1931.

With the increased use of the automobile after 1930 and the expansion of suburban neighborhoods after World War II, the Durant and Farm Hill districts underwent a period of growth. Hunting Hill Avenue was extended to Randolph Road during the late 1950s and single-family houses were built throughout the neighborhood. Strip development, including gas stations, grocery stores and restaurants occurred along South Main Street to provide services for the expanded community.

Maromas

Maromas is located in the southeastern part of Middletown, near the Haddam border.

Lyman Baldwin posed on Main Street with a team of oxen, circa 1915. Behind him is the west side of Main Street, just north of Grand Street. He was a farmer in East Long Hill, on what is today known as Arbutus Street.
Courtesy Kelsey Family

By the 1930s, Route 15 (now Route 17), which cut through Long Hill, served as a major route between New York and Boston. The Cypress Grill was opened by Jimmy Carta, in 1936, as a diner and bus station for travelers along the busy road. "Every weekend the Cypress served *approximately 240 customers every 20 minutes . . . accommodating such renowned celebrities as Benny Goodman, Cab Calloway and Lawrence Welk."* *(Cypress Menu)*
Courtesy J. Russell "Doc" Ward

This photograph of the A. M. Colegrove house on Wadsworth Street, taken in 1892, illustrates the dual nature of West Long Hill as an agricultural neighborhood that incorporated many high-style residences. Although Colegrove was the director of the First National Bank and owner of the McDonough Hotel until his death in 1895, he was equally well known for his prize-winning cows, which freely roamed the lawn of his estate. Built in 1868, the Second Empire style house, constructed of brownstone, still stands, although minus the tower and belfry. From Parish, Scenes of Middlesex County, courtesy Greater Middletown Preservation Trust

The westernmost part of Maromas became the Hubbard and Haddam Road school districts in the 1870s. Initially known by its Indian name, Regowset, Maromas developed a strong relationship with Middle Haddam during the eighteenth century due to its remoteness from Middletown center. Overland travel was extremely difficult; most residents of Maromas attended church at Knowles Landing, a part of Middle Haddam, that was accessible directly across the river by ferry beginning in 1736. Attendance at Sunday services was required by law in the eighteenth century, and several services were held throughout the day. Those who traveled to Middletown for church needed the financial means to build "Sabbath Day Houses" nearby, in order to rest between services.

The residents of Maromas were primarily farmers. Although Middle Haddam provided a better launching place for ships, some trade was carried on in Maromas. In addition to surplus grain and wheat, fish and lumber were shipped from local docks. The ships were owned by Middletown merchants, but Maromas had at least two active sea captains during the eighteenth century. Beginning in 1820, granite quarries provided jobs in Maromas. Although Maromas granite was of rough quality, with traces of iron, it served well for foundations, bridges, and monuments. Until the opening of "Quarry D" in 1885, all the work at the quarries was done by hand. "Great yokes of oxen hauled the stone to the docks, by means of the old two-wheeled quarry carts, from the axle of which the stone hung suspended." (WPA, 1937) Quarry D installed expensive machinery for quarrying and put in tracks to deliver the stone to the nearby railroad line. Quarrying stopped abruptly about 1905, when concrete became widely used. As the old families left the area at the turn of the century, immigrants, anxious to return to the farming life they had known in Europe, bought Maromas farms. Maromas became home to German, Swedish, and Polish families who rejuvenated its farmlands and homesteads.

In 1956, the core of the village, on the Connecticut River, was demolished for the construction of the Connecticut Advanced Nuclear Engineering Laboratory (C.A.N.E.L.), a United States government project. River Road, which originally ran from Middletown's center to Higganum, was sealed off, making the district accessible only by winding interior roads. Mrs. Florence Gilbert, who was born in Maromas and attended the one-room school there, has described the subsequent changes in the area: in the 1970s, trying to show a young relative the old family homelot on River Road, she was unable to recognize the neighborhood because it had been reclaimed by the forest. C.A.N.E.L.'s property was acquired in 1966 by Pratt and Whitney Aircraft, part of United Technologies, at present one of Middletown's largest employers. □

Colonel Clarence Seymour Wadsworth built the elegant "Long Hill" estate in West Long Hill from 1909 to 1917. Designed in the Beaux Arts style, the house has a two-story central main block with flanking two-story wings. Four full-height Greek Revival columns, of the Doric order, support the projecting portico, which is highlighted by a circular driveway. Wadsworth removed the columns from the Nehemiah Hubbard, Jr., House, also part of his wife's inheritance, that stood on Main Street until 1986, when it was torn down to make room for an addition to Farmers and Mechanics Savings Bank. The land surrounding the mansion, the Little Falls and Laurel Creek sections of Middlefield and Long Hill, were transformed into a park by Wadsworth with the creation of country lanes and fieldstone arch bridges. The mansion was sold by the Rockfall Corporation in 1945, at which time it was converted to a religious retreat, known as the Cenacle. It was sold to developers in 1986, but plans for the vacant estate are, as yet, uncertain.
Courtesy City of Middletown Commission on the Arts and Culture

Tucked away in the southwestern part of Long Hill is the Wadsworth Falls State Park, a rural area along Laurel Grove Road and Forest Street that provides a serene escape from the twentieth century. The beauty of the roadways is enhanced by the absence of utility poles, which Wadsworth had, ingeniously, installed underground. The Potters Lane Bridge, shown here, is an S-curve concrete arched bridge faced with fieldstone, built by Clarence Wadsworth on his estate. The lane approaching the bridge, bordered by a fieldstone retaining wall, is one of several trails meandering through the wooded park.
Modern photograph courtesy Rockfall Foundation

In 1915, Dan Michelli, Ludwig Hoffman, Ben Larson, Jack Shittick, and foreman Art Sage used muscle and ingenuity to raise a utility pole on Long Hill Road, in front of the main building at Long Lane School. This part of Long Hill experienced the most growth after 1860 because of its proximity to Middletown's center.
Courtesy Doris Hoffman Lee

After the establishment at South Farms of the Sanseer Mill in 1832 and the Russell Manufacturing Company in 1833, a commercial/residential neighborhood developed along East Main Street and Saybrook Road. The trolley line, shown here at the intersection of Chestnut and East Main streets, provided easy access to and from the district. On the left is St. John's Evangelical Lutheran Church, established in 1901 and later called Grace Lutheran. Courtesy Anne Toczko Nowakowski

The "thousand and one things needed for the household" were sold at Mrs. M. A. Smith's Grocery Store at the corner of East Main Street and Saybrook Road. An article about the store in 1890 claimed that it was unnecessary for the residents of South Farms to ever have to travel into the city for their needs ("Leading Business Men . . ."). Smith's grocery, which opened in 1868 and occupied this brick facility in 1890, had five teams of horses delivering groceries all over Middletown. The structure was torn down in the mid-1980s. From the 1896 Middletown Tribune Souvenir Edition, courtesy Mrs. Helen Raffuse

The Bow Lane district of South Farms was a rural farming community that, after 1866, abutted the property of the Connecticut Insane Asylum. Georgiana (Lord) and John Talcott Scovill, shown here in 1915 with five of their eight children, moved from Johnson Lane to Bow Lane with the help of their two oldest boys, Fred and Talcott Scovill. The boys had picked huckleberries to earn the $2 needed to buy a pair of oxen from the Lee Farm in 1909. They then trained the oxen, sold them, and received enough money for their parents to put a down payment on the property at Bow Lane. Courtesy Barbara Melia

Lawrence and John Scovill, the two youngest sons of Georgiana and John Talcott Scovill, enjoyed the natural offerings of the Bow Lane district in 1925. Courtesy Barbara Melia

About 1905, the town built a new district school, shown here in 1911, for the residents of Johnson Lane, on the present Millbrook Road. The school also provided the rural farming community with a public hall, augmenting the Millbrook Road Lyceum, which was used for dances, riding club meetings, and parties. Today, the school serves as a dwelling on the east side of Millbrook Road, just north of Daniels Farm Dairy.
Courtesy Mrs. Willard Hubbard

This photograph of the interior of the first Johnson Lane School, about 1900, illustrates the rustic environment in which the children of Middletown's farming communities were educated. Rural schools usually followed the schedule of farmers; spring and autumn were for planting and harvesting, not for reading and arithmetic. When the new schoolhouse was built, this building was moved further south on Millbrook Road, to property presently owned by Lewis Daniels, where it now serves as a garage and barn.
Courtesy Mrs. Willard Hubbard

Sherman Bailey opened this meat market on Ridge Road, near the head of Russell Street, about 1900. David and Joseph Dripps (center and right, respectively) bought the store in the twenties and posed here with store employee, Fred Scovill (left) in 1929. On the night of January 21, 1939, Joseph Dripps was killed by two armed robbers while closing the store. The people of Middletown were "aroused to a high pitch," (Middletown Press, January 23, 1939) and demanded justice for the two men arrested for the crime, Ira Allen Weaver and Vincent Cots. Cots and Weaver were tried, convicted, and hanged within six weeks of the murder. Courtesy Barbara Melia

In 1871, this new schoolhouse on River Road became the Maromas district's primary public building, used for church services and social affairs. Six grades and about twenty students attended the one-room school, seen here in 1910. The building was torn down about 1956 by the Connecticut Advanced Nuclear Engineering Laboratory (C.A.N.E.L.). Courtesy Florence B. Gilbert

Ridge Road was laid out upon the ridge across Farm Hill at South Farms, and was originally known as High Street. This photograph was taken about 1910, looking south from near Russell Street.
Courtesy Gerald and Lorraine Augustine

The year 1871 saw the opening of the Connecticut Valley Railroad between Hartford and Saybrook. Maromas lay on the path of the Valley Line, providing villagers with easy access to Middletown, Saybrook, and Hartford. Seen here is the Maromas Station about 1940. It, too, was destroyed about 1956.
Courtesy Colonel C. B. McCoid

For almost one hundred years this farmstead on River Road in Maromas was home to the Bailey family. When this photograph was taken in 1915, the Baileys ran a dairy farm. This house was razed by C.A.N.E.L. in 1956 when they built their facilities at the end of what is now Aircraft Road.
Courtesy Florence B. Gilbert

Bear Hill Road winds through the interior region of Maromas in 1935. On the right is the home built by the Dornfried family in 1927 on the site of a Colonial home that had belonged to the Butler family. Early residents of Maromas, the Butlers lent their name to the district's principal stream that feeds the numerous reservoirs in Maromas. This 1927 house still stands and is owned by the Schilke family.
Courtesy J. Russell "Doc" Ward

141

The Middletown-Portland Bridge, 1985.
Courtesy Rick Mazzotta, Dark Eyes Images

5

Entering the Modern Era
1900 and Beyond
❏

A New Century

As Middletown entered the new century it celebrated the 250th anniversary of its founding. Optimism for the future and pride in the past characterized the mood of the community and of the nation at the turn of the century. The city's population was 17,464 in 1900; with the continued influx of European immigrants, it had increased to almost 21,000 by 1910. Never had life seemed so good. Ushered in by the Gay Nineties, the period from 1890 to 1920 was "the age of the trolley car, the bicycle and the brass band." (*Middletown Tercentenary*, 1950) Bicycles were all the rage as a way to good health and relaxation. Robert Keating, of Springfield, Massachusetts, built a factory on North Main Street in 1897 to produce his superior bicycle (later the factory was occupied by Remington-Rand). The Keating Wheel Works manufactured the first motor-driven bicycle in the United States. The Eisenhuth Horseless Vehicle Company operated from the same building, and produced 384 automobiles between 1904 and 1906. The preceding decades of industrial and commercial prosperity in Middletown had established a growing middle class which devoted more of their time to leisure activities. On weekends, families picnicked at Lakeview Park (today Crystal Lake), bicycled to Westfield Falls, and attended theater productions, such as *Robin Hood* and *Rip Van Winkle.* ☐

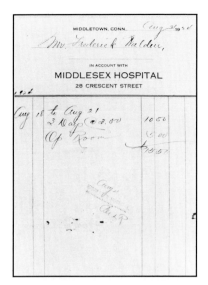

The Middlesex Hospital opened its doors in 1904, and its physical facilities expanded for the next seventy years. When Frederick Walden of Chester received this bill for $15.50, which covered his three-day stay and the charge for use of the operating room, the hospital had recently spent $1,200 for steam laundry equipment and its payroll was over $7,000 a year. In 1924, the hospital became one of the first in the state to have a private supply of radium, at the cost of $7,500 for sixty milligrams, and used it within the year to treat over a hundred patients for cancer.
Courtesy Mrs. Helen Raffuse

The invention of the automobile at the turn of the century created a demand for parts dealers and repairmen. William Fortin, Sr. (right), came to Middletown in 1905 from Union, Connecticut. Seeing that Middletown did not have an automobile parts store to supply the increasing number of car owners, he seized the opportunity to corner the market. His first store was on Rapallo Avenue, before moving to this location at 720 Main Street (next to the present O'Rourke's Diner). Henry Ford started marketing the Model T, known as the "flivver" or "tin lizzie," as the car that nearly every family could afford, and over eleven thousand cars were sold during the first year of production. By 1925, Ford was manufacturing nine thousand cars a day. The number of stores catering to the automotive needs of Middletown increased. The Alling Rubber Company of Danbury opened a branch selling auto parts and tires in 1919. In 1922, Clinton H. Warner and Ellsworth F. Page, both former employees of Alling Rubber, established Page and Warner, Inc., dealers of "Genuine Ford Parts, Auto Accessories, Oils, Greases, Tires and Tubes," on Main Street opposite the national guard armory. (Page and Warner letterhead, 1928)
Photograph, circa 1910, courtesy Bill Fortin

The "Aeroview," such as this one of Middletown in 1915, was a popular format for city maps during the early twentieth century. The Aeroview map provided an opportunity for the city to express its pride in its factories, transportation networks, and commercial operations, and presented an idealized view of Middletown—without slums, industrial smog, or telegraph wires.
Courtesy Wesleyan University Library, Special Collections and Archives

In 1902 Middletown was the home of the Eisenhuth Horseless Vehicle Company. The Eisenhuth car shown here, the only remaining example known to exist, is currently owned by the Magee Company of Middlefield.
Courtesy Magee Company Collection

In the years before and after 1900 the rapid expansion of the economy increased the number of people who, although not rich, were financially comfortable. The middle class found itself increasingly free of old social constraints. President Theodore Roosevelt embodied the spirit of the times. Everything he did was accom-panied by fanfare; he climbed mountains, rode with a posse in North Dakota to capture bank robbers, and performed antics for photographers. It was in this environment that flagpole sitting became a wild craze. As this 1913 photograph illustrates, Middletown was not immune to the antics of the era. The daredevil *balancing atop the McDonough House above the corner of Main and Court streets was Harry A. McLaughlin, the physical director of the local Y.M.C.A. Note the Nickel Theater in the foreground, which had been the McDonough Opera House until 1910.*
Courtesy J. Russell "Doc" Ward

In 1913 the following directive was added to the ordinances of the city of Middletown:

"The city shall have a corporate seal, the device upon which shall be as follows: In the foreground, a railroad locomotive, with implements of agricultural, manufacturing, and mechanical industry; in the middle ground, a river bearing on its surface a steamer and other vessels; and in the background, the rising sun with a landscape . . . which seal shall be kept by the mayor."

The design used on the seal was created many years before it was deemed the official seal, however. References to it, and reproductions of the image, were used as early as 1880.
Courtesy J. Russell "Doc" Ward

The bungalow-style house was popular during the first two decades of the twentieth century. Speculative builders often constructed these small cottages in groups, such as the cluster on Ridge Road south of Russell Street. First built by the English in India, the bungalow came to characterize a new American way of living. The bungalow had a living room, rather than a parlor, which better suited the middle class need for family recreation. Because of the bungalow's close association with a modern style of life, songs were written about them and the life carried on within them. Historians have discovered at least twenty-two songs about bungalows, including this one by Kenneth MacDougall, published locally in 1910. The first verse of the "Bungalow Love Song" was:

Bungalosis is a very funny kind of trouble
That seems to come to people by degrees.
Some have it worse than others
Fact my sister and my brothers to cure it had to go down by the ocean breeze.

Now there's a funny feeling
That o'er me has come a stealing
It's the Bungalosis germ I fear in me.

And I know I must endure it
For the only way to cure it
Is for you to love and fin'lly marry me.

You will have to be the doctor
For I have it bad you know,
And the antidote is you dear and a pretty Bungalow.

Chorus: So in a B-u-n-g-e-l-o double u
I'll l-o-v-e much a girl I know
An In-gle Nook will be a place to spoon,
We'll have a big veranda
Where we'll watch the moon.
And there will be a lake we can go ca-noe-ing
And in winter we'll skate and go snow-shoe-ing.
We won't be rich but we'll be proud to show
All our friends our pretty little Bungalow.
Courtesy Ann C. Street

This building on the north side of lower Washington Street, next to the railroad tracks, served as the first depot for the Connecticut Valley Line from the time of its inception in 1868, until Union Station was built circa 1880. After the custom house on Main Street was razed in 1916 to make way for the post office, this house was converted to a customs building for clearing immigrants traveling by steamer from Ellis Island to Middletown. There, "officials checked the baggages and bundles which consisted of mainly salami, cheese and onions." (Tarallo, 1979) This photograph was taken just prior to the demolition of the building in the late 1940s.
Courtesy J. Russell "Doc" Ward

World War I

Fifteen hundred Middletown people served in World War I (1917-1919), and thirty-seven lost their lives in combat, at sea, or from disease. On the home front, the war caused great hardship with "Heatless Mondays" and shortages of sugar and meat. Many local workers were laid off for one week in 1918 when factories and stores were closed to conserve coal. In that same year a flu epidemic struck. Funeral director Peter O'Callaghan was also overburdened. On one trip through town to collect the dead, he filled the back of his hearse to capacity and propped another corpse in the passenger seat. ☐

Prohibition and the Roaring Twenties

The temperance movement, dating back to the 1830s, was revived with the organization of the Connecticut Women's Christian Temperance Union in Middletown in 1875. Rachel Wilcox, wife of William Walter Wilcox of Wilcox, Crittenden and Company, was its first president. In 1919, this national social reform movement prompted the passage of the Eighteenth Amendment to the Constitution, which prohibited the manufacture, sale, or transportation of alcohol in the United States. This is not to say that the consumption of alcohol ceased in Middletown. Between 1920 and 1930, Middletown police arrested 396 people for violating the Eighteenth Amendment. However, local officials often turned a blind eye to the sale or manufacture of liquor. Many Italians and Poles went right on fermenting wine and gin in their basements. Joyce's speakeasy at Main and Court streets catered to the working class, and Hoffner's on East Main Street served local businessmen. Fraternal clubs, including the Benevolent Protective Order of Elks and the Middletown Rotary

Club, also made liquor available to their members. Twenty-one members of the Wesleyan University student body were reprimanded during Prohibition for illegal use of alcohol, and eight were dismissed. Liquor was smuggled in from Jamaica and Europe by way of the river. According to a patrolman on the Middletown police force during Prohibition, it was well known that bootleggers used the basement of the New England Enameling Company on River Road as a warehouse. (Schorr)

The prosperous and happy times following World War I came to be known as the Roaring Twenties. Yet, immediately after the war, the people of the United States were uneasy. The economy seemed headed for a depression when industries that had geared up for the war effort saw a decline in demand for their products. Many of the nation's fears were put to rest when Calvin Coolidge was elected in 1924 on a pro-business platform. It was during this period that many of Middletown's clubs for business people were organized, such as the Middletown Rotary Club, the Kiwanis Club of Middletown, and the Chamber of Commerce.

During the twenties, as the economy was revived, Middletown began to enjoy the luxuries of a new age. One of the most important forces shaping daily life was the automobile. Henry Ford perfected the assembly line form of mass production, enabling him to cut the cost of his Model T to $290 by 1925. With the average family making about $3500 a year, it became possible for most families to own a car. Automobiles stimulated road construction and spawned new businesses, such as service stations and parts and tire stores. Distribution of electricity also brought about great changes in everyday life. Houses in city neighborhoods were equipped with electric lights by the

147

In 1919, Samuel Russell, Jr., great-grandson of the prosperous China merchant, led the parade down Main Street to celebrate the return of those who fought in Europe during World War I. Russell was a gentleman farmer who spent most of the year residing at his estate in Westfield, on Ridgewood Road. was active in the Westfield community and was the catalyst for the formation the Westfield Consolidated School in 1 to provide improved educational standards and better facilities for the youth that rural district.

The buildings behind Russell in this photograph were on the east side of M Street, and were part of the Center to College street block. This section of M Street was demolished in 1961. Courtesy J. Russell "Doc" Ward

A total eclipse of the sun occurred on January 26, 1925, and was photographed from atop the post office building, with the tower of the Municipal Building in the foreground. The eclipse was the first since Wesleyan University's Van Vleck Observatory had been built in 1916, providing students and faculty with an opportunity to study its effects. Spear's Department Store and the Mansion Block (with the mansard roof) can be seen in the background, on the east side of Main Street. Courtesy Mr. and Mrs. Howard Thompson

late 1920s, although many farms in rural districts used kerosene lamps into the 1940s. Electricity also changed the appearance of the kitchen, replacing dripping iceboxes with the refrigerator, soon to be followed by the electric washing machine and stove. Radios, 12 million of them nationwide by 1930, brought news, music, and comedy entertainment directly into the homes of Middletown people, along with raucous commercials for shaving soap and holeproof hosiery. □

The Great Depression

The good life of the 1920s was shattered by the Great Depression. Although many Middletown families were devastated economically by the stock market crash in October of 1929, Middletown was not as hard hit by the Depression as other cities in the United States. Many in the middle and upper classes had only begun to make their money ten or fifteen years before the Depression: consequently they were not heavily invested in the stock market. Instead, they had conservatively deposited their wealth in local banks, which did not fail. Workers were hardest hit by the closing

A flood in November of 1927, although not as well known as the flood of 1936, caused 168 deaths in Connecticut and Massachusetts. After a tropical storm from the Gulf of Mexico dropped an undetermined amount of rain, the waters of the Connecticut River rose quickly and violently, eventually bringing the river more than twenty-two feet above flood stage. This photograph shows the water mark below Main Street. A team of horses retrieved this car from Hartford Avenue, near Water Street. In the background, to the left of Hartford Avenue, the houses that once stood at the northern end of Water Street are visible.
Courtesy Wesleyan University Library, Special Collections and Archives

The buildings of the former Allison Brothers Soap Works on Sumner Street, which by 1927 housed Schwacher's Garage and Atlantic Gasoline, were under water during flooding in November of 1927. The buildings were torn down sometime before 1940.
Courtesy Robert Chamberlain

of factories, widespread unemployment, and the bitter labor strikes of the thirties. The Remington Noiseless Typewriter Company, located on North Main Street, was the site of a major industrial dispute in 1936. In 1934 James Rand bought out the company begun by Joseph Merriam, a Middletown native, about 1905. By July of 1936 it became clear to the workers that Rand had no intention of bargaining with the union representatives from the American Federation of Labor. After two years of negotiating for improved wages, a thousand of the twelve hundred employees walked out. Rand hired Pearl Bergoff, the "King of the Strikebreakers," called in replacement workers, and labeled the strikers communists and radicals. Violence erupted between workers and strikebreakers, and the National Guard was called in to restore order. Yet, with support from Mayor Leo B. Santangelo, the Middletown Press, and the National Labor Relations Board, the workers refused to be intimidated into returning to work. James Rand, instead of conceding to the strikers, closed the plant and moved it to New York.

The Mayor's Committee on the Unemployed

raised $23,000 in 1931 to hire four hundred workers to cut wood, and three thousand people in Middletown donated 2 percent of their salary for aid to the poor. After the election of Franklin Delano Roosevelt as president, federal and state aid was available through the Works Progress Administration (WPA), which put people to work building roads and bridges, and landscaping neighborhood parks. The Civilian Conservation Corps was kept busy doing forestry work at Higby Reservoir. The Federal Writers' Project provided employment for local artists, poets, and writers. Historical sketches of Middletown districts were prepared, including an account of Maromas, and a survey of historic buildings in Middlesex County documented the status of existing Colonial period homes. Through the efforts of Russell Manufacturing and Wilcox, Crittenden to keep its employees on the payrolls, Middletown worked its way through the Depression. By 1938, Middletown's commercial center was relatively stable and could still claim to be the "shopping center of Middlesex County." ☐

In 1920, the black population of Middletown had dropped to fifty-seven people, but in the late twenties and early thirties it was supplemented by southern black workers hired by the Tuttle Brick Yards in Newfield. The brick company, established in 1842 by George L. Tuttle, produced high-quality brick used in public and residential buildings throughout New England. Although the steady flow of Italian immigrants into Middletown provided the yards with labor, a shortage of workers before the Depression led the Tuttles to recruit southern black workers. The company built housing for its workers at Yard One (opposite Tiger Lane) and at Yard Four (near Tuttle Road). The Tuttle Yards built and donated a school for the district, which was attended primarily by workers' children. The 1932 class at Newfield School illustrates the ethnic and racial blend of the neighborhood. Pictured (left to right), front row: Daisy Mae Moody, Willie Hunter, and Ruby Lee Hunter; second row: Rita Grassi, Ella Mae Hunter, Yolanda Botti, John Botti, _____ Bonafonti, and Bean Tuttle; third row: Roland LeBlanc, Rocco Botti, Jack Snow, _____ Cronin, Charles Moody, Martha Alvord, and Art

Ghezzi; fourth row: Walter Lineberry, Mary Eward, Ruby Hodge, Norma Broadbent, and Bill Fortin. Baseball was a popular pastime, and a field was laid out across from the school, where the brick-yard workers played out-of-town teams and hosted large parties after the game. Courtesy Bill Fortin

In 1925, the outlying districts organized into the Middletown Consolidated School District and funded the construction of Woodrow Wilson High School (shown here) on Hunting Hill Avenue in 1931. The division of Middletown into the City District and the Town of Middletown in 1784 had caused unequal educational opportunities for those living in Middletown. Before Woodrow Wilson High School was built, students in the outlying districts, where elementary requirements were considered less rigorous than in the city, were required to take an exam before admittance to Middletown High School. Edith Lindholm, later the wife of Governor Raymond E. Baldwin, lived on a farm in Newfield and had attended the one-room school in that district until 1911. "When Edith went to high school, she had to walk from Newfield to Middletown High School and back, regardless of the weather, except when her father hitched

up the horse and buggy and drove her to school." (Baldwin, 1968) With the creation of two high schools in Middletown, a rivalry between the football teams began almost immediately. It lasted until the schools merged in 1984. When a new Woodrow Wilson High School was built in 1954, the old school was adapted for Woodrow Wilson Junior High School. As enrollment in Middletown schools declined, the junior high school closed. In 1987, it was converted to moderately priced apartments. Courtesy Everett Wright

In 1932, the northwest corner of Main and Washington streets housed the F. B. Fountain Company, florists (adjacent to Caulkin's Buick dealership), Blau's Appliance Store, Middlesex Automotive Company, and Max Levin's Fruitery. Fountain's florist shop, begun by Henry Fountain in 1876, once incorporated five hothouses covering five thousand square feet, and was the largest operation of its kind in Middletown at the turn of the century. (It did not come close to rivaling the enterprise of A. N. Pierson in Cromwell, however.) Courtesy J. Russell "Doc" Ward

Part of the City School District, the South Main Street School, in 1929, included the following students (left to right), back row: Arthur Press, Irving Blifford, Jack O'Brien, unidentified, Myer Field, Dick Sweet, Hall Strickland, Edwin Browlow, unidentified, John Wiley, unidentified, Floyd Hubbard, and Fred Clark; middle row: Estelle Shapiro, Muriel Lohneis, un-identified, _____ Larsen, Phyllis Langer, Dorothy Hill, _____ Wagner, _____ Wagner; first row; four unidentified boys, Barbara Molander, Betsy Hurlburt, Patricia McCarthy, Raymond Petrofsky, and three unidentified boys. The school building, adapted for use as a residence, still stands near the corner of Cottage Street.
Courtesy Barbara Molander Warner

Jack's Lunch had been a popular diner on Main Street since 1922. Located on the east side of the street, near Washington Street, Jack's Lunch was known through-out the Northeast as the inventor of the steamed hamburger and also for its bawdy advertising brochures. This interior view of the diner was taken in 1933.
Courtesy J. Russell "Doc" Ward

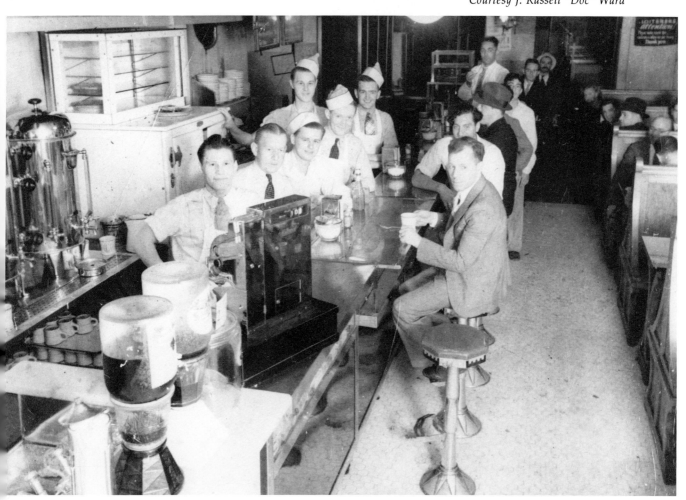

In the early thirties, Jack's Lunch sponsored Angelo Magnano and Jigger Daniel's
cross-country roller skating journey from
Middletown to Los Angeles. The two men
ran out of funds in New York.
Courtesy James Inferrera

Works Progress Administration foreman
Daniel Clark posed at WPA headquarters
on County Lane off Court Street in 1933.
Workers hired by the WPA laid out new
roads in rural areas, including part of
Bartholomew Road in the Hubbard dis-
trict, Hillside Road in South Farms, and
Barbara Road off Old Mill Road. They
improved older roads like Bear Hill and
River roads in Maromas, and Highland
Avenue. The Municipal Field on Farm
Hill Road (now Pat Kidney Field) was
cleared and leveled for three baseball
fields, several tennis courts, and horseshoe
courts. Old stone culverts and wooden
bridges were replaced by metal drains
and concrete bridges on East Street,
Ridgewood Road, and Lyceum Road.
The bridge built over Sumner Brook on
Russell Street by the WPA served the
community until it was rebuilt in 1988.
Many of the stone walls along Middle-
town's roadways and most of the monuments in public parks were installed by
WPA workers during the 1930s.
Courtesy Warren and Elvira Lee

When the Twenty-first Amendment was passed, repealing Prohibition, liquor stores reopened and restaurants began serving alcohol again. The arrival of one of the first shipments of alcohol to Middletown, in 1933, was a memorable enough occasion to have been recorded. Here, Tony Spada unloads beer from the delivery truck in front of Max Levin's store, formerly located at the site of Caulkin's Restaurant parking lot. Courtesy J. Russell "Doc" Ward

The Hotel Riverview, shown here about 1933, was opened by John and Louise Hudec, and their partners Charles and Francis Houska, in the Laurel section of Maromas in the late 1920s. The summer resort catered primarily to a New York clientele who sought to escape the city for a week or two of country life. The vacationer could dine and dance, play tennis, and swim in the Connecticut River from the adjacent docks. The hotel was damaged during the flood of 1936 and subsequently closed. During the 1950s, the Middletown Station of Connecticut Light & Power Company, a subsidiary of Northeast Utilities, was built on the site of the former hotel. Courtesy Colonel C. B. McCoid

Leo A. Combe leaned on the new company truck at his Silver Street home in 1936. Four years earlier he had opened Standard Tire Company at the northwest corner of Main and William streets and ushered in the new era of the clean, efficient service station. Although Middletown already had a few gas stations, most were small, usually with only one pump, and only sold gasoline. Carl Schilke's station at Saybrook Road and East Main Street in South Farms, which opened in 1921, was one of the earliest in Middletown. Standard Tire, which sold Texaco brand gasoline, occupied a large lot and offered full service at its pumps. Service attendants wore "puttees," leather leggings over knickers, to give them a clean, uniformed appearance as they pumped gas, cleaned windshields, and checked the air in the tires. Tires were sold and minor repairs, such as lubrications and oil changes, were offered in the garage. In the late thirties a Mobil station opened down the street, just south of the Baptist Church, and a Gulf station was built on the former site of the Middletown Savings Bank at the southeast corner of Main and William streets. Standard Tire remained in business, operated by Leo Combe's four sons, until 1967. The Redevelopment Agency moved its offices into the former garage for two years before razing the building. Courtesy Katherine P. Combe

A diver emerges from the Connecticut River after working on the bridge. A coffer dam was constructed in order to prepare part of the base for the massive granite and concrete piers, and caissons were used to provide pressurized chambers for workers cutting through solid rock to make way for the bridge's foundation. Working under air pressure of 45 to 47 pounds, laborers were only allowed to work for three-quarters of an hour before they decompressed for an equal amount of time. Five hours of rest were required before they returned to work. Divers were required for underwater work in lowering the caissons and for drawing steel cables across unspanned areas. For almost three years, work on the bridge was carried on twenty-four hours a day.
Courtesy John Irving Anderson Family

A new bridge between Middletown and Portland was begun in 1936 and completed in 1938, replacing the drawbridge built in 1896. Constructed only a few yards north of the first bridge, seen here in the foreground, the new span was named for Senator Charles J. Arrigoni of Durham, chairman of the bridge committee. The bridge opened in August 1938, only two months before the great hurricane of that year. The older bridge was removed within a year after the hurricane. This photograph was taken from the railroad bridge, just south of the two passenger spans.
Courtesy John Irving Anderson Family

Flooding during March of 1936 brought the river to its highest point in recorded history. After rain had already brought the rivers above flood stage in early March, the rains came down again for three full days. The river crested almost forty feet above flood stage. Factories and businesses were forced to close and more than one hundred families in Middletown fled their homes and sought refuge in the state armory or American Legion Hall. The town was without electricity for over a week and the Middletown-Portland Bridge was closed because of heavy debris piled against its foundation. North Main Street, shown here, was flooded by waters from both the Connecticut and Sebethe rivers. Remington Rand is in the upper right corner. In the foreground are the warehouses for Meech and Stoddard, Inc., a flour and feed business that was established in 1871.
Courtesy Wesleyan University Library, Special Collections and Archives

Floods and a Hurricane

The most serious blows dealt Middletown during the first forty years of the twentieth century were struck by nature. The year 1927 brought the worst flooding in memory, which claimed hundreds of lives throughout New England. A tropical storm dropped heavy rains in November, swelling the rivers and streams more than twenty-two feet above normal and forcing many in Middletown to evacuate the low-lying areas for several weeks. Forty million dollars in damage was done in New England. Although the Flood of '27 came suddenly and violently, its highest water mark could not compare with that of the Flood of '36. Beginning on March 11, on the forty-eighth anniversary of the Blizzard of '88, the rains began slowly, stopped, then began again and did not stop for three full days, eventually raising the waters of the Connecticut and Sebethe rivers almost forty feet above flood state. (A line drawn to record the water's highest level was visible until recently on the concrete retaining wall along Hartford Avenue.) Homes were swept off their foundations, and thousands were forced to evacuate as the waters invaded. Debris piled up alongside the foundation of the Middletown-Portland Bridge, forcing it to shut down for several weeks. The town was isolated and without electrical power.

Barely had Middletown time to recover from the flood's damage when it was struck by the "Great New England Hurricane" of 1938. Winds of over 170 miles per hour hit without warning at 3:15 P.M. on September 21, devastating Middletown. Nineteen cows were killed at Guida's Farm on Coleman Road when a hay-filled barn collapsed on them. Although Middletown did not suffer any loss of human life, seventeen people were killed in other parts of Middlesex County, and hundreds of homes were damaged or destroyed. The hurricane had been preceded by several days of rain and flooding that had already collapsed bridges and dams, and inundated inland areas, including Randolph Road and Mill Hollow. With the ground soaked by the rains, trees throughout Middletown were uprooted during the hurricane, causing most of the town's damage. "Historic old trees that shaded the walks of every street in what was last Wednesday a veritable forest city," were levelled in a matter of minutes, changing the appearance of Middletown for several decades. (The *Middletown Press*, October 1, 1938) Wesleyan University, noted for its tree-lined campus, was one of the areas most severely damaged. Flooding continued for several days after the hurricane, bringing the waters to within two feet of the 1936 high-water mark. □

The tenements housing many of Middletown's poorest people, east of Main Street and along Bridge Street, suffered the most damage in the Flood of 1936. Here, residents survey the damage to residential properties that were adjacent to the railroad tracks between lower Court and College streets.
Courtesy John Irving Anderson Family

"The Great New England Hurricane" took Middletown by surprise on September 21, 1938. St. Sebastian Roman Catholic Church on Washington Street, shown here the morning after the storm, lost several stained-glass windows and most of the trees on its grounds. Middletown was already flooded from several days of rain when the hurricane struck without warning. The residents were unprepared for the winds that smashed inland, estimated at 180 miles per hour.
Courtesy Greater Middletown Preservation Trust

South Main Street was lined with tall oak and elm trees, which caused significant damage as they fell during the Hurricane of 1938. This photograph was taken in front of the Hoberman family apartments, on the hill opposite Crescent Street. The hurricane also brought 9.5 inches of rain in a forty-eight hour period, causing extensive flooding near the river and along the streams in the interior of Middletown.
Courtesy Colonel C. B. McCoid

In 1939, Middletown was visited by the Florida Hoboes baseball team. Part of the semiprofessional baseball league, the Hoboes traveled on a playing circuit that brought them to the area for games against the teams of the Middlesex League. Baseball was an important pastime in the 1940s, drawing up to four thousand people a game at the Municipal Field (Pat Kidney Field). The Hoboes' stay was prolonged when the team ran out of money, and by 1941 the team had split up. Local baseball enthusiasts convinced several of the Hoboes to try out for local teams. Four of them made the Middletown Giants, and appear in this 1944 photograph; front row, second from left, Earl Baker; third from left, Larry Matthews; fourth from left, Curly Ready; and back row, second from left, Fletcher Henry. Henry, Ready, and Baker found work at Wilcox, Crittenden and Company through the efforts of the team's business manager, Jack Rybczyk, and Phelps Ingersol, manager of Wilcox, Crittenden. Ingersol agreed to hire the men for the second shift, with paid time off for evening games, provided they returned to work afterward. The former Hoboes drew large crowds who came to Middletown Giant games to see the "Sepian players' . . . abilities and their vaudevillian antics." (undated Middletown Press article, 1941) They led the Giants to county championships from 1943 to 1947. Baker, the team's pitcher was named Most Valuable Player in Middlesex County in 1944. Matthews had left Middletown by 1945, but Baker, Ready, and Henry married local women and stayed in Middletown. In the back row, seated third from left, is Middletown Giants' general manager Jack Rybczyk. Fifth from the left is teammate Bernie O'Rourke, a primary figure in the Middletown sports scene for most of his life. He served as director of Middletown's recreation department beginning in the 1940's and was director of the parks and recreation department until the 1980s. He was best known as sports editor for the Middletown Press. Courtesy John Rybczyk

World War II

Everyone in Middletown had a stake in the outcome of World War II. The descendants of immigrants, particularly, sought to remove the threat of Fascism from their ancestral homelands and to repay America for the opportunity it had afforded them. At least thirty-seven hundred men and women from Middletown served in the war, in Europe and the South Pacific. At home, the war effort meant sacrifice. High school students collected scrap metal, bought war stamps, and listened to air raid lectures. Women, many with small children, found themselves coping single-handedly with the challenges of daily life. Many children born during the war were two or three years old before they met their fathers. Blackout curtains in windows protected the town from possible air attack, and butter, eggs, sugar, and meat were rationed. "A" cards restricted families' monthly allotment of gasoline. Women, who had comprised only 25 percent of the work force in 1941, increasingly found work outside the home during the war. Many housewives and young women just entering the work force took jobs at factories and government organizations. Russell Manufacturing Company waged a campaign to employ women, primarily to sew and weave industrial belting. A sign in their shop in 1943 advertised women's contributions to the war effort: "The Army Recognizes the Dependable Skill of a Woman's Hands—And Heart." Many black families relocated from Southern states to Middletown between 1941 and 1945 to find employment in factories where the war had depleted the supply of workers. □

On Friday night, August 30, 1941, a fire started in the kitchen of Frankenberger Cafe on Court Street (the present site of Valentino's Cafe), a busy restaurant owned by John Bransfield. Less than five hours later the east side of Main Street, from Court Street northward to the Palace Theater (the present Middletown Area Transit station), was destroyed. Nine buildings and twelve businesses, including Barton's Clothing Company, State Wine and Liquor, First National grocery store, Central News, and Pelton and King Publishing Company were gone. Thousands of people, many of whom had been out shopping on that Friday night, crowded Main Street to watch the flames and firefighting activities. Firemen battled the blaze all night and were kept busy for nearly a week as flames rekindled in the rubble.
Courtesy Jennie DiGiandominico

Among the first to leave Middletown for World War II was the 43d Infantry Division's Medical Detachment and B Company of the 169th Infantry Division. The troops were housed in the National Guard Armory on Main Street. Approximately three hundred men from the Division travelled by train to Florida where they spent the next year training for combat in the South Pacific. In early 1942, half the division was shipped overseas to the South Pacific, while the others remained in the South as a training battalion. Six Middletown men from the 43d Division lost their lives. In this photograph, the medics of the 43d Division leave from Middletown's Union Station on March 14, 1941.
Courtesy Colonel C. B. McCoid

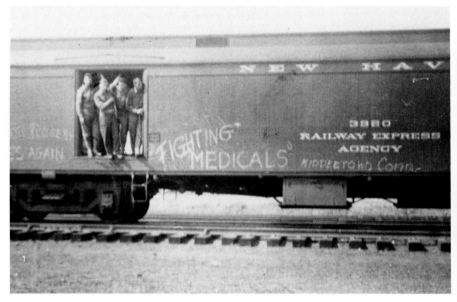

The State Council of Defense administered the war fund from this small building on Main Street, next to the Church of the Holy Trinity. The war fund's goal was to raise $100,000 by selling Liberty bonds. The site, which had been part of the Berkeley Divinity School until 1928, was occupied for a time by a log cabin built for headquarters of Middletown's tercentenary committee in 1935. The tercentenary committee had constructed what they believed to be a representative example of an early Middletown settler's house. Since that time, scholars have dispelled the idea that seventeenth-century families lived in log cabins. After the start of World War II, this building was built for the State Council of Defense. It was razed in the 1950s and replaced by a brick structure, which since 1989 has been occupied by the Middletown Chamber of Commerce and the Middlesex Industrial Development Corporation.
Courtesy Colonel C. B. McCoid

During World War II, Max Corvo of Middletown (seated in this photograph on the right) was the director of Special Intelligence (S.I.) for the Office of Strategic Services (O.S.S.), forerunner of the C.I.A. Max Corvo was particularly suited for the job. His father, Cesare Corvo, had been an anti-fascist forced to leave Italy when Mussolini came to power, and he had provided his son with a rich background in Italian history and politics. Max Corvo gathered intelligence information con-

cerning the activities of the Fascists in preparation for the Allied invasion of Sicily. Corvo recruited many S.I. men from Middletown's Italian-American community because they were bilingual and familiar with Italian ways. Among the Middletown recruits were Sebastian Passanesi, Vincent Scamparino (seated on the left), Emilio Daddario, Louis Fiorilla, Samuel Fraulino, and Frank Tarallo (standing in back row on the left). All were well-educated; Scamporino and Fraulino were trained as lawyers. Passanesi was an architect, and Emilio "Mim" Dadario graduated from Wesleyan University and served as mayor of Middletown, and state representative from the First District, for almost sixteen years. Four other Italian-Americans, not residents of Middletown, also served. The group was told "Don't fight, don't shoot, don't kill" (Tarallo); instead they participated in freeing political prisoners jailed by Mussolini in Sicily, and establishing military bases throughout the Mediterranean area in preparation for the invasion. Courtesy Max Corvo Collection

Middletown factories adjusted immediately to producing for the war effort after 1941. With the loss of workers to the armed services, the factories were constantly in need of laborers. Through advertisements, such as this one from the Russell Manufacturing Company, both men and women were recruited to work. Rusco, as Russell Manufacturing was known, manufactured belting and brake linings for trucks and jeeps, as well as webbing for machine guns and tanks. Courtesy Sheila B. Moulson

During World War II, women worked jobs formerly reserved for men. In this 1944 photograph, Rita Comb (later Mrs. Charles Hazel) and her sister-in-law, Peggy (Cunningham) Combe, were pumping gas at Standard Tire on Main and William streets. Courtesy Katherine P. Combe

In 1947, the James H. Bunce Company sponsored the first landing of a helicopter on an American Main Street. Schools were closed and Life magazine was present to record the event. James German (center of photograph with light-colored coat and hat), a manager at Bunce's and the son-in-law of Richard Bunce, had served in the Navy Air Corps during World War II. The helicopter was a new phenomenon, and a war buddy of German's (pilot in uniform) promoted the use of helicopters for Sikorsky Aircraft. The two friends arranged to have a helicopter land in front of City Hall on Main Street, pick up the mayor, Emilio Dadario, and then land again in Bunce's parking lot. For two weeks before the event, raffle tickets were sold to Bunce's customers for a free ride over the river and the city of Middletown. Courtesy Greater Middletown Preservation Trust

The Postwar Era

When the veterans returned to Middletown after World War II, their expectations for their future, and for the future of Middletown, had changed. Advances in automobile design from technology developed for combat vehicles, along with improved highways, led to a more mobile population. People looked beyond Middletown for employment, relocating to distant cities or traveling daily to Hartford and Meriden for jobs in large corporations. In 1950, there were approximately 12,000 persons working in Middletown. By 1954, the number had risen to 13,000, but over 2,000 residents commuted to jobs out of town. New limited-access highways, such as Acheson Drive (Route 9), begun in 1950, made commuting relatively easy. For those who lived in Middletown, the car allowed them to live further from their places of work, resulting in the development of suburban neighborhoods far from the central business district. Rows of one-family houses were built, with the garage as a dominant feature, along streets such as Hunting Hill Avenue, south of Russell Street, and Fisher Road, off Westfield Street. The housing boom in suburban areas instigated a need for commercial services close by residential areas. Strips of grocery stores and gasoline stations developed along Washington Street and South Main Street to fill the need. In the 1950s, federal funds made available by the Housing Act of 1949 were used to construct Long River Village on Silver Street to meet the overwhelming need

for moderate-income units. Veterans were able to buy homes with government mortgage programs and to attend college on the G.I. Bill. So confident was Middletown in its future that, in 1943, discussions were initiated concerning the building of an airport as a central facility for the state. Sites were considered in Newfield (near Mile Lane), Maromas, and Westfield. A feasibility study proved Middletown's location in a valley inappropriate for air traffic.

After World War II, Middletown maintained a solid, although modest, economic base. The sixty-five manufacturing and industrial enterprises in Middletown provided 15 percent of the tax revenues. Although several factories closed in the 1960s, including the Goodyear Rubber Plant with 1,200 employees, new industry moved in. Pratt and Whitney Aircraft, a division of United Technologies, bought Connecticut Advanced Nuclear Engineering Laboratory plant (C.A.N.E.L.) in Maromas in 1966 and within a few months hired 1,350 workers.

Corporations were also added to the city's tax base during the 1950s. American Education Press of Columbus, Ohio, was purchased by Wesleyan University in 1952 and provided employment for thirty white-collar workers at its Washington Street headquarters. This periodicals company, established in 1907, published Current Events, Weekly Reader, and Read magazines for the elementary and junior high school market. In the early sixties American Education Press moved to its new facili-

In 1952, President Harry Truman and his daughter, Margaret, visited Middletown and addressed a large gathering in front of the Main Street City Hall. Truman, who had chosen not to run for a second term, urged the Middletown citizens to vote for Adlai Stevenson, the Democratic party candidate running against Dwight D. Eisenhower. Behind Truman on the platform are, left to right, Margaret Truman (to the right of the flag), Democratic Party Town Chairman John Tynan (behind her with glasses), Senator Abe Ribicoff (to the right of Truman's shoulder), and Congressman William M. Citron.
Courtesy J. Russell "Doc" Ward

ties at 55 High Street, and was subsequently sold to the Xerox Corporation in 1965. The company built new headquarters on Long Hill Road in 1971. The company was bought out in 1985 by The Field Publications, a publishing and direct marketing firm based in Chicago, Illinois, and remains one of Middletown's top fifteen employers, with a staff of three hundred.

Even before the war, Middletown needed improved school facilities and better-organized school districts. In 1959, Middletown voted to merge the Central (downtown) and Consolidated (outlying) school districts under one superintendent and one board of education. This eliminated testing of children in the outlying areas before they entered Middletown High School, and removed the burden of financial support from the Consolidated School Board. Several elementary schools were built during the 1950s, including Wilbert Snow School in Westfield and Bielefield School in South Farms, to meet the needs of the growing population in the suburbs and the postwar baby boom.

Through the efforts of Wilbert J. Snow of Middletown, the state of Connecticut established a system of regional colleges in 1965. Middlesex Community College opened in 1965, a branch of Manchester Community College. The first classes were held at night at Woodrow Wilson High School, but in 1968, the school broke ties with Manchester, and by 1973 had a campus of its own on land donated by the state from its holdings at Connecticut Valley Hospital. ☐

In 1950, Bernie Fields moved to Middletown from Long Island and bought Pinsker's Jewelry Store, which had been in business since 1903. In 1955, he relocated the store from Main Street near the corner of College Street, to its present Main Street location just north of Court Street. At that time he changed the name to Bernie Fields Jewelers. Bernie Fields has been active in Middletown community life since he arrived. He started the Big Brothers program in Middletown during the 1960s and has sponsored numerous baseball teams.
Courtesy Bernie Fields

Some Notable Men

As part of the tercentenary celebration of the founding of Middletown, these notable Middletown men were brought together on April 17, 1950, for an informal radio program on WCNX radio station. In the studio, left to right, are Dr. Edward C. Acheson, Jr., Chief of Police John L. Pomfret, Secretary of State Dean G. Acheson, Lieutenant Edward J. Hill, and Judge Raymond E. Baldwin. The Acheson brothers were sons of Edward Campion Acheson, who served as rector of the Church of the Holy Trinity in Middletown from 1892 until 1915, when he was consecrated the Episcopalian Bishop of Connecticut. Dean Gooderham Acheson, born in 1893, served as assistant secretary of state under President Franklin Delano Roosevelt beginning in 1941, and as secretary of state during Harry S. Truman's administration. His brother, Dr. Edward "Teddy" Acheson, was a professor at George Washington University. During the tercentenary celebration in 1950, Acheson Drive, which was incorporated into Route 9 later in the fifties, was dedicated in honor of Dean Acheson's national contributions.

Raymond Earl Baldwin, born in Rye, New York, called Middletown home. Baldwin became the only person to serve Connecticut as governor, United States senator, and chief justice of the state supreme court. He was elected governor in 1938 and 1942, bringing a liberal, youthful Republican party back into office after ten years of Democratic control. He came to national prominence when he delivered the seconding speech for Wendell Wilkie at the Republican National Convention in 1940. After four years as a United States senator, Baldwin accepted an appointment to the Connecticut Supreme Court, upon which he served for the next thirteen years, including four years as chief justice. Baldwin was a much-admired statesman who possessed a friendly and direct personal style. At Middletown High School he was active in theatrical performances and served as chairman of the student council and president of his senior class. Summers were spent working in Portland tobacco fields or at the New England Enameling Company. During the school year he worked Saturdays, from 7:00 A.M. to 11:00 P.M., at a Main Street clothing store for $1 a day. After his retirement in 1965, Judge Baldwin and his wife, Edith Lindholm Baldwin, made their home in Middletown, where he died in 1986.
Courtesy Middletown Press

Redevelopment

If a person living in Middletown in 1954 suddenly found himself on the corner of Main and College streets in 1984, the view would be almost unrecognizable. In those thirty years, urban renewal transformed downtown. As part of Harry S. Truman's Fair Deal in 1949, state and federal aid was made available for communities to undertake urban renewal. Many cities used the federal aid to demolish tenements and older industrial buildings, perceived as "urban blight." All that was old was considered substandard, and cities across the country wanted to update the appearance of their urban streetscapes to mirror the modern technological age. Middletown was determined to raze the crowded residential neighborhoods east of Main Street.

When Wesleyan professor Stephen K. Bailey was elected mayor in 1952, Middletown faced several dilemmas. Commercial growth along Route 66 (Washington Street) and Route 17 (South Main Street) threatened the city's commercial and retail center, Main Street. Mayor Bailey attempted, unsuccessfully, to pass restrictive zoning laws barring large retail properties outside the downtown area and also sought to increase the number of parking lots on and near Main Street. Six and a half acres—several city blocks between the river and Main Street—were targeted for renewal.

Redevelopment was implemented in several phases over the next thirty years. The first phase involved the razing of all buildings and roadways along the river in the early 1950s for construction of Acheson Drive (Route 9). In 1957 the second

When Stephen K. Bailey was elected mayor in 1952, the development of shopping strips along South Main Street and Washington Street threatened the prosperity of Main Street. To repair the decaying image of Main Street, he persuaded the city to enter a phase of redevelopment that would rebuild Middletown as an urban showcase. Bailey's plans for the redevelopment of Main Street and the waterfront, reproduced here, called for demolishing all existing buildings in the 6.5 acres bounded by Main Street, the river, and William and Court streets. His vision was carried out, almost exactly as he perceived it, over the next thirty years. Courtesy Wesleyan University Library, Special Collections and Archives

phase was undertaken when the northwest corner of lower Court Street was chosen as the site for the new Municipal Building, adjacent to the State Superior Court. The third phase was the demolition of two full city blocks in 1960—the south side of lower Court Street, the north side of lower College Street, and all buildings along Center Street where Riverview Center now stands.

The congested area along Court, Center, and College streets was slated for demolition owing to substandard housing, and health and safety problems "beyond remedy and control." Mayor Bailey, returning to Middletown to address the Chamber of Commerce in 1971, claimed personal observation—the view from his mayoral office—as a motivating factor for demolition of this area: *The mayor's office in the old City Hall . . . was on the fourth floor overlooking the dilapidation between Main Street and the River. The scene was a daily depressant . . . I had made fire inspections with Frank Dunn, and had seen and smelled the dismal overcrowding. I had cruised the area at 2:00 A.M. with Johnny Pomfret [Middletown's Chief of Police] . . . and had seen and had picked up derelicts and drunks . . . I knew that the concentration of our urban pathology was within the four blocks that I could see from my office window. I knew that slums were cancerous.*

Three-quarters of the dwelling units in the Center Street area did not have central heat, and half were without piped hot water. The area was demolished in 1961 and Riverview Center was built on the site. Its primary tenants were the First National grocery store and the Sears and Roebuck Company. Federal law required that the Redevelopment Agency find suitable living accommodations for all families displaced by urban renewal. Mayor Bailey stated in his 1953 redevelopment report that "there is every expectation that sufficient adequate private rentals will be found for families

Center Street, which ran between College and Court, had traditionally been the site for most of Middletown's livery stables, and the area was infested with rats. Most of the structures were two- or three-story wooden buildings, which housed the influx of immigrants in the late nineteenth century. Photographed here in 1960, the block was razed within a year. One hundred and eighty-three families, twenty-two single persons, and twenty-eight businesses and organizations were displaced by its demolition. Courtesy Wesleyan University Library, Special Collections and Archives

Urban Development (HUD), it closely mirrored the plans established by the Redevelopment Agency in the fifties. The northwest corner of William and Main streets was cleared for Sbona Tower and its adjacent park in 1969, and in the early seventies the west side of Main Street south of William Street was demolished. Through the efforts of John F. Reynolds III, three historic buildings slated for demolition in other downtown areas were moved to this block and converted to professional office space. Beginning in the early seventies, houses and businesses along Union Street, behind the present Y.M.C.A. facilities, were razed along with the residential neighborhood on Sumner and South streets to the east. Parking lots for the *Middletown Press*, the Y.M.C.A., and the Middlesex Memorial Hospital are located in the cleared area.

It was not until the fifth phase of redevelopment plans threatened the South Green that the residents of Middletown began to question the rapid destruction of their community's historic resources. Plans called for slicing off a large portion of Middletown's only remaining nineteenth-century downtown park in an effort to straighten South Main Street and open it to five lanes of traffic. In 1972, the Greater Middletown Preservation Trust was formed, a non-profit advocacy

Demolition of the east side of Main Street, between Court and College streets was well underway when this photograph was taken in 1961. Only the buildings that fronted Main Street remained. Route 9, in the background, was partially opened in the early fifties, and completed in the early sixties, eliminating River Road to Cromwell.
Courtesy Middletown Press

When the two blocks had been cleared, a large parking lot remained. By 1962, Riverview Center was constructed where Center Street had once been. It was occupied by Sears and Roebuck Company and the First National grocery store as primary tenants. Note that City Hall on Main Street had already been razed. City offices had been moved into the Municipal Building on DeKoven Drive by 1959.
Courtesy Middletown Press

displaced from the project areas.'' For those qualifying for entry into public housing he cited the availability of 190 federal low-rent units and 126 state moderate-rental units scattered throughout Middletown, including the housing at Long River Village that had been built as veterans' housing after World War II. In addition, 162 new moderately priced rentals were being constructed with state funds on Long Lane and Wadsworth Street. The Redevelopment Agency also provided financial assistance to help pay for moving expenses and duplicate rent payment in hardship cases.

The South End was targeted as the fourth phase of renewal in the late 1960s and early 1970s. Although the project in the South End was part of the urban renewal project and was sponsored by the United States Department of Housing and

group devoted to preserving the historical and architectural resources of the region. The Trust filed lawsuits against the Redevelopment Agency and the city of Middletown and halted the destruction of the green. With the support of the community and, ultimately, through cooperation between the Redevelopment Agency and the Greater Middletown Preservation Trust, rehabilitation replaced removal on Middletown's streets. The last major demolition occurred in 1978 on the east side of Main Street, from College to William streets, including the razing of the 1826 Mansion Block, to make way for Metro Square. The Redevelopment Agency was disbanded in 1984 and reorganized fifteen months later.

During the 1980s, adaptive re-use of older buildings became financially feasible through federally funded programs, such as the Community Development Block Grant Program and the Local Public Works Program, which provided assistance for private and public developers rehabilitating older commercial and industrial buildings designated as historic. The North End, which had escaped redevelopment during the sixties and seventies, was targeted for rehabilitation in the 1980s. HUD-assisted rehabilitation programs have brought substandard mixed-use (commercial and residential) structures up to modern building and safety codes and restored facades to their original architectural style. □

The South End Restoration Project

In 1976, the west side of Main Street south of William Street "was occupied by a vacant lot choked with weeds, a brick ten-family tenement, a pizza palace, a combined Honda dealership-gas station-taxi service and the Baptist Church." (New York Times, September 25, 1977) One year later, three historic houses graced the block, and all other buildings except the Baptist Church had been demolished. In an effort to save a part of Middletown's architectural heritage from the destruction he had witnessed for twenty years, John F. Reynolds III, a founder of the Greater Middletown Preservation Trust, moved the three houses from various downtown locations to the block between Church and William streets. The Redevelopment Agency, which had planned to put apartments on the property, endorsed Reynolds's proposal at a time when the public was awakening to the loss of the town's historic fabric. But it was four years before Reynolds overcame all the obstacles threatening the project. For example, fire regulations prevented new or restored wood-frame buildings on Main Street. In 1975 Reynolds received a waiver from the City Council that would exclude the three houses from the downtown fire district. Financing the project, Reynolds bought the houses for $1 each when they were slated for demolition in 1972 and also bought the land for under $26,000. Although he anticipated a return on his investment through the rental of the professional office space, Reynolds's main concern was saving the buildings as part of Middletown's history. Special covenants were included in the deeds of sale from the Redevelopment Agency to ensure accurate restorations, protecting the houses from alterations until the year 2009.

The three historic buildings, shown here in a 1990 photograph, were originally built in very different settings. The building on the left, at the corner of Main and Old Church streets, was built in 1771 for Caleb Fuller on the site of the present Baptist Church. Fuller was a preacher, town constable, school master, and part-time innkeeper. Before the Baptist Church was built in 1842, this gambrel-roofed Colonial-style house was moved west on William Street, where it remained in residential use until it was bought by the Redevelopment Agency in 1975. Reynolds's restoration of the house included the addition of a front entry porch from the 1788 Captain Magill House on Union Street, which had been destroyed by fire in 1975. The paneling in the parlors came from a 1777 house that was demolished by the Redevelopment Agency.

The Reverend John Cookson, pastor of the Baptist Society in Middletown, built the house in the center of the photograph, in 1837 on a half-acre lot on the west side of South Main Street, where doctors' offices at 80 South Main Street now stand. Blending elements of the Federal and Greek Revival styles, this transitional building represented a conservative architectural statement for its time. The doorway, with its rectangular sidelights and overlights, reflects the more modern Greek Revival style of the period, while the delicate ornamentation and the gable fanlight are remnants of the Federal style. Five owners subsequently occupied the house after Cookson sold it in 1847 and before the Redevelopment Agency bought it in 1972. The Cookson House was the first of Reynolds's three buildings to be moved to its new site in 1977, and it seems appropriate that the home of a former pastor is now adjacent to the new Baptist Church.

The oldest of the three houses is the large center chimney Colonial house on the right. It was begun by William Southmayd in 1747 on the south side of lower William Street. The family owned land east of Main Street, from William to Court streets. William died before the house was completed, and his widow, Mehitabel, completed it. About 1800, the house was updated to reflect the new Federal style of architecture, and the original facade with three window openings on each floor was altered to five openings at each level. The delicate columned entrance porch was also added at that time. The Southmayd family owned the house until 1825, when it was sold to Lot D. VanSands, a Middletown manufacturer. For most of the twentieth century, the house served as a multifamily dwelling until acquired by the Redevelopment Agency in 1975. Reynolds was able to restore the house with much of its original fabric. The original stairway, with its turned spindles and carved handrails, was restored, as was a hidden cupboard discovered in the wall of the staircase.

John Reynolds also restored the Charles Boardman House (across the street from the three buildings and north of the Middletown Press building). As these restorations went forward, local people were surprised to learn that the building known until 1980 as the White Eagle Cafe, with its modern neon sign and glass commercial facade, was in actuality a center-chimney Colonial house built in 1753. The interior retained many original features, including a stairway with turned balusters and newel posts, paneling in several rooms, and four fireplaces. Beneath the shingles on the exterior were hidden early clapboards. Reynolds also undertook the restoration of the vacant barn behind the White Eagle Cafe, which had served as a chandlery for West Indian trade goods beginning in 1758. Both the Charles Boardman House and the chandlery were sold to Reynolds by the Redevelopment Agency in 1979.

By the late 1970s, large-scale urban renewal was being reconsidered. Instead, existing commercial buildings were rehabilitated as mixed-use projects with commercial space on ground level and apartments above. Federal and state funding sources were tapped by the city to encourage the rehabilitation of the historic fabric and scale of the North End, shown here in 1984. The view is of the east side of Main Street, from Master Industrial Supply, Inc., on the right, to St. John's Roman Catholic Church.
Courtesy Greater Middletown Preservation Trust

"When the G.O.P. got tired of losing the city elections in Middletown they put up for mayor a fine Italian businessman named Santangelo, and he swept the city." (Snow) That first Italian-American mayor was Leo B. Santangelo, who was elected for one term in 1934. Santangelo was not of Melillese descent. It was not until 1969, with the election of Mayor Buddy Sbona, that the first descendant of Melillese immigrants held Middletown's highest office. Mayors since that time, including the present mayor, Paul Gionfriddo, shown here in City Council chambers, have been able to trace their ancestry to Melilli, Sicily.
Photograph by Matt Polansky

Political Leadership

Beginning in 1784, the year that Middletown was incorporated as a city, local government was structured much as it is today. The people elected a mayor and councilmen (women and black freemen were denied the right to vote). These public offices were preceded by those of town clerk, first appointed in 1711, and city surveyor, first elected in 1715. Jabez Hamlin was Middletown's first mayor, and his office was located in the court house that stood at the corner of Court and Pearl streets. Even in the nineteenth century, the city council played an important role in the government of the city. It represented the interests of Middletown's general population and determined the outcome of issues ranging from zoning to tax abatements and economic development. It was not until the tenure of Philip Roth in 1961 that Middletown's mayoralty became a full-time job. Roth had retired from Pratt and Whitney Aircraft and therefore was able to commit all his time to his city responsibilities.

Beginning with the election of Mayor William T. Elmer in 1876 and continuing with Willard C. Fisher in 1906, Wesleyan University has provided several of Middletown's mayors, including Stephen K. Bailey who led the city through redevelopment in the 1950s. Others affiliated with the university entered into broader spheres of politics, including Professor Wilbert Snow, who served as lieutenant governor in the 1940s, and James L. McConaughy, a former president of the university elected governor of the state in 1946. In the late nineteenth century the efforts of several Wesleyan students to obtain the right to vote in local elections caused a controversy among townspeople, who feared student votes might swing the election away from candidates who would better represent Middletown's majority. This issue was raised again in 1989, when heavy turnout from the Wesleyan

voting district led to the perception that the Wesleyan vote helped defeat a two-term mayoral incumbent.

For almost four decades, Middletown politics were controlled by one man—John Tynan. An old-fashioned political boss, Tynan was Democratic town chairman from the early twenties until the sixties. Tynan "enjoyed doing favors for people, some of which had strings attached to them: others did not. He insisted on getting much gravy for himself and his inner circle of friends. But when a need of the town was at stake, John could be counted on." (Snow, 1968) Tynan served as Middletown's tax assessor, an appointed position he held throughout his career. He and a small circle of state men hand-picked mayoral, gubernatorial, and senatorial candidates for the Democratic tickets. Tynan's dominance in city affairs came to an end when the Italian-American population asserted its political power in 1969 with the election of Mayor Anthony "Buddy" Sbona. Italian-Americans representing both the Republican and Democratic parties have served as mayor since that time.

The Turbulent Sixties

"We [black students] recognize the dialectical relationship which exists between the educational system which de-values and de-historicizes Black people by consciously ignoring the accomplishments and contributions of their forebearers to the American tradition, and the political and social system which rejects and oppresses them by depriving them of their rights as American citizens . . . Education is a tapestry woven of many threads and we repudiate any system which seeks to favour one strand over the composite of the whole."

Thus began the statement prepared by the black students who took over Wilbur Fisk Hall at Wesleyan University in February of 1969. After

Local civil rights protesters demonstrated on Main Street in early 1963 calling for federal troops to be sent to Birmingham, Alabama, to protect the black community from racial violence. The National Association for the Advancement of Colored People (NAACP) organized Middletown's march, that drew primarily white activists. In this photograph, the marchers are headed north on the east side of Main Street. The intersection of William Street is in the center.
Photograph by Larry Marino, courtesy Middletown Press

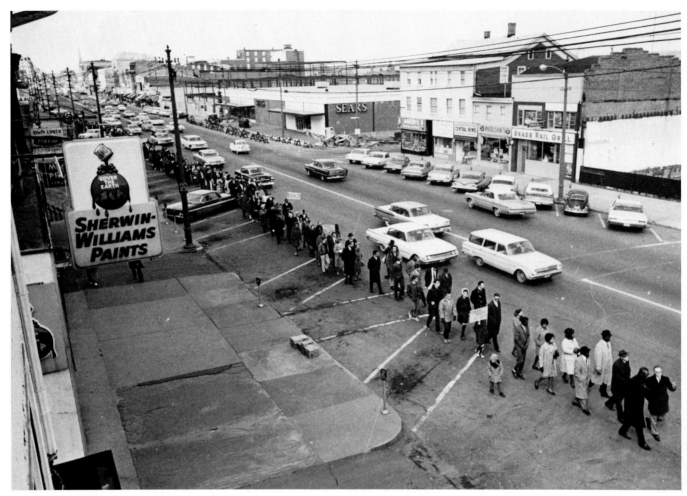

On March 14, 1965, civil rights demon-
strators peaceably marched down Main
Street on the way to the South Green after a three-day conference on civil rights
held at Wesleyan University. Three hundred protesters, representing organizations such as the Congress on Racial
Equality (CORE), Students for a Democratic Society (SDS), Student Non-Violent
Coordinating Committee (SNCC) and the
Northern Student Movement, were joined

by more than one hundred Middletown
citizens along their Main Street march.
The conference, attended primarily by
white activists, focused on civil rights
violations in the South, particularly the
use of literacy tests as a requirement for
voting in Alabama. Less than two weeks
earlier, a peaceful march across the
Edmund Pettrus Bridge in Selma, Alabama, had been broken up by state police
using clubs and tear gas. The day was

dubbed "Bloody Sunday," and communities across America, like Middletown, responded by organizing marches calling for
federal troops to be sent to Selma. After
the Middletown march, several participants from Wesleyan left for Selma to join
the thousands of Americans who continued the demonstrations.
Photograph by Louis Marino, courtesy
Middletown Press

the administration refused to call off classes to
commemorate the fourth anniversary of the assas-
sination of Malcolm X, more than forty of Wesleyan's ninety-two black students barricaded
themselves inside the building at the northeast
corner of High and College streets, which then
housed the university bookstore, post office, and
several classrooms. They were joined by a group
of black students representing Middlesex Community College and the local high schools. Wesleyan
president Edwin D. Etheridge responded by can-
celing classes and scheduling discussion groups on
campus to provide students with an opportunity
to vent their concerns. At 4:00 P.M., when university classes regularly ended each day, the occupying students peacefully left the building and

marched to the Center for Afro-American Studies
on High Street.

Until the 1940s, Middletown's black population had been small; only fifty-three blacks lived
in the city in 1920. During the mid-twenties, several families relocated from the south to work in
the Tuttle Brick Yards on Newfield Street, and
integration into the city of that small community
had occurred quietly. During World War II, the
city's black population increased. Charles Ghent
came to Middletown from Florida in the early forties, one of the first blacks to work at Connecticut
Valley Hospital. He and the one other black
employee had to eat separately from white employees in an outbuilding on the farm. Charles
Ghent fought for and attained access to regular

A Connecticut River tugboat tows a freight barge past Middletown's harbor. In the background is the vacant Middletown Yacht Club, built in 1906, and to its right, the 1918 Connecticut Power Company generating plant. When this photograph was taken in 1979, both buildings were owned by the city of Middletown. The yacht club stood vacant and the generating plant was used by the city's Park and Recreation Department. At this time, plans were already underway to convert the waterfront area to a public park with the construction of a boardwalk along the river's edge and landscaping of the adjacent land. In 1982, the generating plant was demolished and the yacht club was renovated by Frank Maratta, Jr., for a restaurant, which opened in 1984. Docking facilities have since been constructed alongside the restaurant, and on summer days numerous boats dock while their owners enjoy the sun and refreshments on the deck.
Courtesy Middletown Press

employee housing at the hospital for the growing number of black workers. During the next thirty years Ghent actively fought discrimination in Middletown, serving as president of the Middletown Branch of the National Association for the Advancement of Colored People, founded in 1943. Ghent applied for admission to, but was rejected by, several of the business and fraternal organizations in Middletown, and in the sixties he sought the integration of Middletown schools which had become segregated owing to discrimination in housing.

The black population composed 10 percent of Middletown's thirty-five thousand people in 1970 and was concentrated in the south end of town, near Union and Sumner streets. (This area, where Connecticut Rental Center is now located, was completely demolished in the mid-seventies.) Equal housing became the primary issue concerning the black community during the fifties and sixties, particularly after urban renewal displaced many black homeowners and tenants. Even after the Civil Rights Act of 1964 made it illegal to discriminate on the basis of race, many black families had difficulty finding adequate housing.

Before and after the take-over of Fisk Hall at

The federal Economic Recovery Tax Act of 1981 encouraged developers and investors to rehabilitate income-producing properties. The tax act helps make the costs of adaptive reuse projects, for industrial, professional, retail, or residential rental use, comparable with the costs of new construction. The 1840 upper mill of the Russell Manufacturing Company, at the corner of East Main and Russell streets, shown here, was converted to the Sumner Brook Mill Condominiums in 1983 as a tax act project. Several historic properties in Middletown have been rehabilitated under the Economic Recovery Tax Act of 1981, and the subsequent updated tax act of 1986. Forge Square on South Main Street was completed in 1988, a conversion of the former Wilcox, Crittenden and Company's forge into eighty-one moderately priced apartments. The Arrawani Hotel was rehabilitated for single-room occupancy apartments in 1989, and the Master Industrial Supply, Inc. building was rebuilt after a fire in 1984, all benefiting from the tax acts. Photograph by Cunningham Associates Ltd.

Wesleyan, black students at Woodrow Wilson and Middletown high schools boycotted classes and submitted demands to the administration asking for more black teachers and for courses that dealt with Afro-American history. As a result, twenty-eight students at Woodrow Wilson High School were suspended for missing classes. In the fall of 1969 Middletown schools added ten new black faculty members and several classes in Afro-American history. Black students from Wesleyan University interrupted church services at the First United Methodist Church on the South Green one Sunday in May 1969, at the same time other students were interrupting services in New York, Los Angeles, and Paris. The students stopped the Reverend Albert Scholten's sermon and made a statement to the congregation demanding a half-billion dollars in reparations and a percentage of the church's income because the "white churches were responsible for many injuries done to Black people in America." The students spoke for five minutes and then left peaceably. Several members of the congregation walked out while they were speaking, but many stayed to hear the pastor's comments following the departure of the students. Scholten commented later that "while everyone felt this was an intrusion, they were willing to look [beyond] and try to see what prompts this." (The Middletown Press, May 12, 1969) Many whites in Middletown were anxious to discuss the community's problems and find solutions for them. But others reacted with fear. A cross was burned on the lawn of Wesleyan's Center for Afro-American Studies in March of 1969.

In 1984 St. John's Roman Catholic Church, in conjunction with the Hispanic Ministry for the Diocese of Norwich, sponsored a parade to celebrate the Fiesta de San Juan Bautista (Feast of St. John the Baptist). To mark the feast day of Puerto Rico's patron Saint, participants came from Willimantic, New London, and Middletown. A group of students carried a banner reading, Los Sequidores, St. John's Middle School.—"The followers, St. John's Middle School." The Hispanic population in Middletown doubled between 1970 and 1980, when there were more than a thousand persons, or 2.6 percent of the population, of Hispanic origin or descent. People from Puerto Rico comprised more than half of this group. St. John's Church, and its elementary and middle schools, has organized events with Middletown's Hispanic community since the 1970s.

Courtesy City of Middletown Commission on the Arts and Culture

The fear in the Middletown community was linked to the rise of militant black activist groups throughout the nation. In the mid-sixties many blacks shunned the peaceful, yet gradual efforts for change embodied in the philosophy of Martin Luther King, and allied themselves with the assertive approach of Malcolm X or the Black Panthers. Fear in the white community and frustration within the black community culminated in violence during the summer of 1969 in Middletown, as it did in cities throughout America. On the night of June 27, a black youth was assaulted by three young white men who were driving through an East Main Street neighborhood. Groups of white and black teen-agers clashed at the Middletown Shopping Plaza on Washington Street. A white youth was stabbed, and a group of blacks returned to the South End and smashed the windows of seven white-owned businesses on Union and East Main streets. The escalation of violence on the following two nights led Mayor Kenneth Dooley to order a downtown curfew, the first in Middletown's history. Beginning at 9:00 P.M. on June 30, 1969, all businesses were required to close and people were ordered off the streets from 10:00 P.M. until 6:00 A.M. Policemen were stationed at four downtown locations to stop all cars and pedestrians from entering the area. But that night, the South End exploded—Kelsey's Paper Company on Union Street was firebombed, and subsequently burned, and Jason's Package Store on Sumner Street was looted. The curfew lasted for two nights, and Fourth of July celebrations were canceled. Although the summer ended calmly, it was months before the tension within the community subsided. □

Middletown Today

According to the United States census of 1980 Middletown is home to more than 39,000 people, and predictions for the population in the 1990 census are as high as 46,000. The number of jobs in Middlesex County is growing faster than in any other area in the state. (U.S. Department of Com-

Between 1979 and 1985, almost 4,000 refugees from Cambodia, Thailand, and Laos settled in Connecticut towns, sponsored primarily by religious charitable organizations. Middletown and its neighboring towns received about 125 persons from Southeast Asia. Mao Chhoeun (left) was only seven years old and his brother, Sothy (right), was eleven when they fled with their father from Phnom Penn, Cambodia, in 1978. They walked to the Thai border, where they were later joined by their mother, Pech, and their nine-year-old sister, Mom. The family spent several years in Thailand before relocating to Pittsburgh in 1981 and to Middletown in 1983.
Photograph by Cunningham Associates Ltd.

merce—Bureau of Census) Pratt and Whitney Aircraft, Raymond Engineering, North and Judd, Inc., and other manufacturers are major employers, providing jobs for more than 5,000 people. But employment by manufacturing companies is decreasing, and is predicted to decline 5 percent by 1995. In contrast, the number of clerical and professional jobs is expected to grow by almost 40 percent in five years as more service corporations locate in Middletown and nearby towns. Institutions such as Middlesex Memorial Hospital and Wesleyan University continue to contribute to the vitality of Middletown's economy. The decision of the 150-year-old Middlesex Mutual Assurance Company to build its corporate headquarters in downtown Middletown represents confidence in the city's future.

Since World War II, Middletown has successfully made the transition from a manufacturing-based economy to a service-oriented one. The change in the social composition of Middletown has developed along national trends. The extended family networks of grandparents, parents, and children with long-standing relationships in the community, has been increasingly supplanted by a more mobile population of single people or nuclear families.

Located midway between New Haven and Hartford, Middletown has become an attractive alternative for homeowners and developers. Various projects are being considered that will greatly impact the downtown area. The construction of a

new courthouse, the expansion of present municipal space, and the establishment of a cultural center will attract more people and new retailers to Main Street.

Wesleyan University has significantly enlarged its campus since the 1930s, and currently incorporates ninety structures, including academic buildings, dormitories, athletic facilities, and libraries. Although new construction in the 1960s added important university buildings, including the Science Center on Church Street (1965, 1971) and the Center for the Arts (1967-1973), Wesleyan's primary growth has been through the purchase of existing buildings in the residential areas surrounding the campus. Most of the high-style nineteenth-century houses on High Street, once the homes of prominent merchants and industrialists, were bought by Wesleyan after 1930. Since that time, Wesleyan has adaptively reused many of its properties on High Street, from Lincoln Street to Highland Avenue, as well as on the side streets running east to Broad Street, from Washington to William streets. Wesleyan's most recent project is the new sports complex on Cross Street.

Middletown today, as it has been for the past three hundred years, is poised to meet the challenges of the future. Just as the city has successfully met the challenges of the past, it will continue to meet those of the twenty-first century. ☐

The Middlesex Mutual Assurance Company, begun in 1836 at the back of a jewelry shop on Main Street, is now housed in downtown's tallest building. Middlesex Mutual's corporate headquarters moved in September of 1989 to this twelve-story office complex at the southeast corner of Court and Broad streets. A seven-level parking garage adjoins the east side of the buildings, and future plans call for another office tower at the corner of College and Broad streets. The insurance company, which employs almost four hundred people, is one of Middletown's ten largest employers. Middlesex Mutual Assurance Company's commitment to the growth of Middletown is expressed by its participation in community activities, such as fundraising for the United Way and the Cromwell Children's Home.
Photograph by Matt Polansky

This central block between Court and Washington streets is the commercial core of downtown. The strongest anchor on Main Street has been Bob's Stores, which draws its customers from throughout the state. Bob's, which now has three branch stores in Connecticut, owes its original success to the popularity of blue jeans in the 1960s. R. J. "Bob" Lapidus, who opened the Gob Shop in 1954, first sold surplus army and navy clothing and survival gear. After opening Bob's Surplus in 1955, he quickly recognized the potential market for blue jeans and carried a wide selection of sizes and styles. Since the seventies, he has expanded the store to carry fashionwear for men and women at reasonable prices. Middletown residents tell of meeting people in the farthest corners of the United States, or even abroad, wearing Bob's teeshirts, who know of Middletown, Connecticut, as the home of Bob's Stores.
Photograph by Matt Polansky

Wesleyan University's award-winning expansion and restoration of its Olin Memorial Library is shown in two views. The $10 million project, dedicated in 1986, features a 40,000-square-foot addition that presents a gently curving north wall to Wesleyan's Andrus Field, site of baseball and football games. The addition has been praised by Architecture magazine as forming "a new layer of the building's skin, wrapping around the old and preserving it as part of a blithe and light-filled interior." The interior view shows the original north facade, designed in 1939 by McKim, Mead and White as the rear wall of an addition to the 1928 library. That facade has been the traditional backdrop for Wesleyan commencements. The facade is now the interior wall of the Colin and Nancy Campbell Reference Center, dedicated in 1989 in honor of Wesleyan's president emeritus and his wife. The project has received awards for its architects, Perry, Dean, Rogers and Partners of Boston, and for Wesleyan. The most recent and most prestigious is one of the seven 1989 Awards of Excellence for Library Architecture, presented jointly by the American Institute of Architects and the American Library Association. According to the jury, "The project gives a sensitive response to both the original library and the surrounding campus . . . (and) makes the original library better in every way." Courtesy Wesleyan University

Watercolor view of Middletown from the Portland shore by Anne Watkinson Welles in 1799.
Courtesy Middlesex County Historical Society

Samuel Russell had this silk coverlet made in China, sometime between 1818 and 1831, while he was a merchant importing Turkish and Bengal opium into Canton and exporting fine Chinese teas and silk to Europe and the United States. Photograph by Larry Ploude, courtesy Ted Bertz Designs and Connecticut National Bank, permission coverlet custodian Thomas M. Russell III

This 1988 painting, Middle Haddam, 1823, *commissioned by a resident of Middle Haddam, depicts the former vitality of Knowles Landing. At one time part of Middletown, the village of Middle Haddam had six shipbuilding yards that produced hundreds of ships and brigs. In the foreground, the ship* Chancellor *is shown hoisting her sails.*
Courtesy Richard and Cynthia Patterson, with permission of the artist Richard L. Brooks

The Children of Nathan Starr, *is an 1835 oil painting by Ambrose Andrews. Nathan Starr's prosperous sword and pistol mill operated from 1812 until 1845. His home, the setting for this painting, stood on High Street where the DKE fraternity is now located.*
Promised gift to Metropolitan Museum of Art in memory of Nathan Comfort Starr (1896-1981), printed with permission from its anonymous owner

Most girls in their early teens completed a sampler as proof that they had mastered needlework. In 1832, Alma Eliza Crowell chose the Arawana Mills as the subject of her sampler. She stitched the mill buildings (at the bottom of the sampler), the alphabet in two types of stitch, and several adages.
Courtesy the Kelsey Family

This view from Cromwell, on the road leading to Middletown, was drawn by John Warner Barber and included in the 1846 volume of his Connecticut Historical Collections. The caption with the engraving reads, "The above view is from Prospect Hill, about 3 miles from the central part of the city (Middletown), on the Hartford Road. In the distance is seen the windings of Connecticut River, the city of Middletown, part of Portland, and its quarries, on the eastern side of the river."
Courtesy Middlesex Mutual Assurance Company

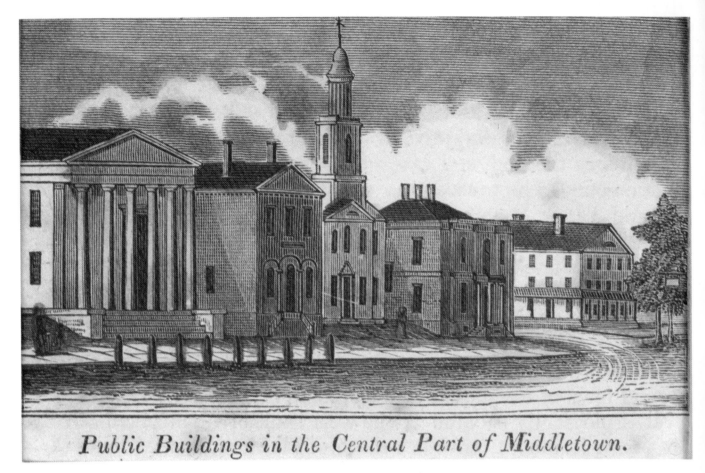

Public Buildings in the Central Part of Middletown.

John Warner Barber, born in 1798, traveled throughout Connecticut sketching the state's scenes in towns and cities. In 1836, Barber published reproductions of wood engravings made from his pencil sketches in the first volume of Connecticut Historical Collections, which was followed by seven volumes over the next ten years. He also issued engraved reproductions of his drawings, many of which were hand-colored, that were sold locally. Shown here is John Warner Barber's engraving of Middletown's public buildings on Main Street. From left to right: the 1832 court house (before the steeple was added), the Middletown Bank, the First Congregational Church, the 1834 Custom House, and Central Hotel (which was razed in 1851 for the McDonough House). Courtesy Rushford Center, Inc., J. Russell "Doc" Ward Collection

This polychrome block print from a piece of wallpaper dating from 1830 has been framed to preserve it from further damage. The lettering reads, "University at Middletown Connecticut Wesleyan, Camps Palestine Garden." From 1828 to 1833, Heth Camp, the owner of several acres of land on the east side of High Street, cultivated a large pleasure garden at the northeast corner of High and William streets that included plants from Palestine in the Middle East. Camp charged an admission fee to wander through the gardens and use the private warm baths offered on the grounds. In 1833, the gardens were removed when Isaac Webb built his house and preparatory school for boys on the site. Courtesy Wesleyan University Library, Special Collections and Archives

O. Vincent Coffin, treasurer of the New Haven, Middletown and Willimantic Railroad Company, signed these investment bonds issued between 1872 and 1875. The railroad was later known as The Air Line, and provided passenger and freight service between New Haven and Willimantic by way of the 1872 railroad bridge across the Connecticut River.
Courtesy Richard Mozdiesz

This broadside from about 1880 advertised an evening of entertainment sponsored by Wesleyan University. The highlight of the program was the Temperance Ballad Singers.
Courtesy Wesleyan University Library, Special Collections and Archives

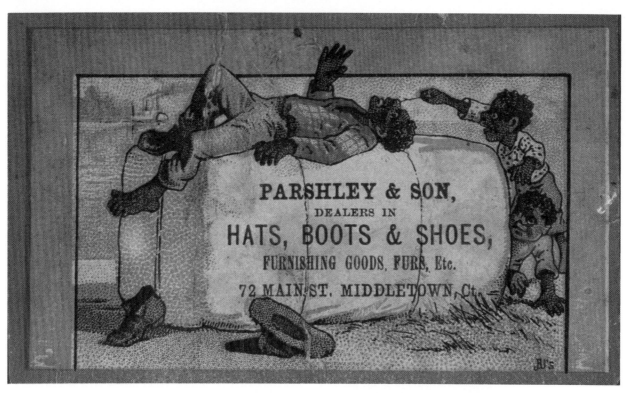

This business card is from Parshley and
Son which was located in the former
Mansion House hotel in the late 1870s.
Anthony R. Parshley bought the Mansion
House in 1878 and renamed it the
Clarendon House.
Courtesy Mrs. Helen Raffuse

The Rockfall Woolen Company began
manufacturing blankets in 1882 in the
factory in the Staddle Hill section of
Middletown once used by Simeon North
for the production of firearms. A label
used by the woolen company in the late
nineteenth century is shown here.
Courtesy Colonel C. B. McCoid

KEATING BICYCLES · 1897
365 DAYS
AHEAD OF THEM ALL

The Keating Wheel Company of Middletown, begun in 1897 by Robert Keating, manufactured bicycles at a plant (later Remington Rand) on North Main Street. In 1900 the company produced the first motor bicycle in the country. The Indian Motorcycle of Springfield, Massachusetts, often described as first, was not patented until 1902.
Courtesy Brian and Gary Keating

Postcards were a popular way to send greetings to Middletown people away from their familiar surroundings. Street scenes and individual houses were reproduced for black-and-white or hand-colored postcards beginning about 1900. Sometimes the same photograph was used for ten or more years, new details enhancing or updating the image.

LANDING A CATCH OF CONN. RIVER SHAD AT MIDDLETOWN, CONN.

Landing a Catch of Conn. River Shad at Middletown, Conn., *postmarked 1910. Courtesy Everett Wright*

Main St., South Farms, Middletown, Conn.

The heart of South Farms, at the intersection of what are today Saybrook Road and East Main Street. On the left is the neighborhood chapel affiliated with Christ Church, and on the right is the brick building of M. A. Smith Grocery Store. In 1910, when this card was postmarked, Main Street did not continue straight along Crescent Street to Saybrook Road. Instead, Main Street turned left along what is today Union Street. It then followed the path of the present DeKoven Drive and East Main Street. It was not until the 1930s that Main Street Extension was put through, connecting Main Street to Saybrook Road. *Courtesy Everett Wright*

Main Street at Night, *postmarked 1915.* *A daytime view of Main Street, taken from William Street looking north, was* *colored to create the appearance of nighttime. On the right is the Crescent Theater's neon sign near the southeast corner* *of Main and Court streets.* *Courtesy Everett Wright*

MIDDLETOWN, CONN. South Park.

The South Green was known as South Park in 1915, and had been called Union Park after the Civil War. In this postcard, a woman strolls across the park headed *east toward the intersection of Main and Union streets.* *Courtesy Everett Wright*

Middletown, Conn. A Winter Scene.

A photograph of the South Green in summer was "winterized" for a run of color postcards about 1908. A trolley makes its way through the snow on Church Street, toward South Main Street.
Courtesy Everett Wright

Standardized postcards were mass produced then adapted for specific cities. This postcard, illustrating what happens "when extremes meet in Middletown, Conn.," was postmarked in 1911.
Courtesy Everett Wright

When "extremes meet in Middletown, Conn."

Middletown, Conn. Bird's Eye View of Pameacha District.

The ice house on Pamaecha Pond is seen from a hill near Highland Avenue, looking southeast toward the Durham Road (South Main Street).
Postcard, postmarked 1911, courtesy of Everett Wright

Lakeview Park in the South Farms district was a popular retreat for weekend picnics and swimming. Beginning in 1895, trolleys provided service to the park from almost everywhere in Middletown. The lake, a boathouse, and a pavilion are visible in this postcard, dated 1912. The lake is currently called Crystal Lake, and the park on Prout Hill Road, shown here, is owned by the Polish Falcons, Inc.
Courtesy Everett Wright

The Lake, Lakeview Park. Middletown, Conn.

Are you having a surprise party out ther Ruth

The German-American societies of several area communities gathered for their first annual ball in 1915 in Middletown and produced this committee ribbon to commemorate the event.
Courtesy Oscar G. Lenz Family

The Palace Theater was built on Main Street in 1916 by Salvatore Adorno, and was originally known as the Grand Theater. One year later, the theater had this backdrop painted. The forty-foot long and twenty-foot wide canvas served not only as an attractive background for musical and dramatic productions in the theater, but provided advertising space for local businesses. In 1922, when the theater was converted to a cinema house, it was renamed the Adorno Silver Palace. The backdrop depicts Main Street, looking south from several yards north of Court Street. City Hall can be seen on the right.
Courtesy City of Middletown Commission on the Arts and Culture

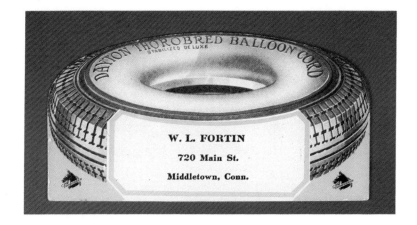

Before ball point pens, ink blotters were needed on every desk. William L. Fortin distributed ink blotters, like the one shown here, to his customers during the 1920s.
Courtesy Bill Fortin

In 1933, the Middlesex Mutual Assurance Company had this mural painted on the lobby wall of its headquarters at the northeast corner of Court and Broad streets. The montage of Middletown scenes included a scene from Fort Hill overlooking the bend in the river and the center of the city at the top, and a reproduction of a late-eighteenth century painting that shows the city from the Portland shore, on the bottom. The scenes in the center, adjacent to the seal of the city, represent distinctive Middletown streetscapes. They are, clockwise starting at the upper left: the buildings on the west side of Main Street, between College and Court streets, in 1833; view looking northeast on Main Street toward the corner of Court Street in 1933; the court house on the west side of Main Street about 1835, and the Middlesex Mutual Assurance Company's headquarters built in 1928. This photograph was taken from a poster made and distributed by Middlesex Mutual after the mural was completed.
Courtesy Middlesex Mutual Assurance Company

189

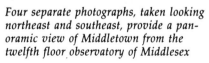

Four separate photographs, taken looking northeast and southeast, provide a panoramic view of Middletown from the twelfth floor observatory of Middlesex

Mutual Assurance Company's new head-quarters at the corner of Broad and Court streets.
Photographs by Matt Polansky

This panorama is the southwest and northwest view from Middlesex Mutual

Assurance Company's observatory. Photographs by Matt Polansky

Industrial development during the 1970s and 1980s has altered the rural appearance of the Westfield section of Middletown. This aerial view of Westfield, taken in the fall of 1989, shows the number of industrial buildings and housing developments in the district. Aetna Life & Casualty Company's Employee Benefits Division on Middle Street is visible in the lower right corner.
Courtesy Middlesex Industrial Development Corporation

Bibliography

❑

The most important primary and secondary source works used in the preparation of this book are cited here. The majority of the primary source materials are available in the Middletown Room of the Russell Library in Middletown, Connecticut.

Anderson, Ruth O. M. *From Yankee to American: Connecticut 1865 to 1914.* Chester, Connecticut: The Pequot Press, 1975.

Annino, James Vincenzo. *Arrivederci Melilli . . . Hello Middletown: A Concise History of the First Families from Melilli, Sicily, to Settle in Middletown, Connecticut, U.S.A.* Hartford, Connecticut: Magnani Press, 1980.

Atkins, Thomas. *History of Middlefield and Long Hill.* Hartford, Connecticut: Case, Lockwood and Brainerd Company, 1883.

Bailey, Stephen K. "Urban Renewal: Then and Now." Address delivered for the Greater Middletown Chamber of Commerce, 1971.

Baldwin, Raymond E. "Judge Baldwin Reminisces." Paper read at Annual Meeting of the Middlesex County Historical Society, Middletown, Connecticut, April 1968.

Baldwin, Howard. Interview with author. October, 1989.

Baumer, Reverend Sally, South Congregational Church. Telephone interview with author. March 1990.

Beers, J. H., ed. *Commemorative Biographical Record of Middlesex County.* Chicago: J. H. Beers Company, 1903.

Beers, Clifford Whittingham. *A Mind That Found Itself.* 1908. Reprint. Pittsburgh, Pennsylvania: University of Pittsburgh Press, 1981.

Brown , Barbara W. and James M. Rose. *Black Roots in Southeastern Connecticut, 1650-1900.* Detroit, Michigan: Gale Research Company, 1980.

Buel, Richard, Jr. *Dear Liberty: Connecticut's Mobilization for the Revolutionary War.* Middletown, Connecticut: Wesleyan University Press, 1980.

Bushman, Richard L. *From Puritan to Yankee: Character and Social Order in Connecticut, 1690-1765.* Cambridge, Massachusetts: Harvard University Press, 1967.

Camp, Mrs. Burton (Rachel R.) "Sixty Years of the Middlesex Memorial Hospital Auxiliary, 1907-1967." Middletown, Connecticut: Middlesex Memorial Hospital Auxiliary, 1967.

Christ Evangelical Lutheran Church. "Thy Hand, O God: Celebration of the Seventy-Fifth Anniversary of the Christ Evangelical Lutheran Church, 1891-1966." Middletown, Connecticut, 1966.

St. Mary of Czestochowa Church. "Story of the Church of St. Mary of Czestochowa, Middletown, Connecticut, 1903-1983." Middletown, Connecticut: St. Mary of Czestochowa Church, 1983.

City of Middletown. "Municipal Yearbook, 1953-1954." Middletown, Connecticut, 1954.

City of Middletown. "Annual Report, 1943." Middletown, Connecticut, 1943.

Congregation Adath Israel's American Bicentennial Celebration Committee. "Middletown Jewry: Then 'til Now." Middletown, Connecticut, 1975.

Connecticut, State Hospital Board. *Report of the Connecticut State Hospital (Middletown, Conn.).* Public Document No. 20. Middletown, Connecticut, 1944.

Connecticut Historical Society. "Black Women of Connecticut: Achievements Against the Odds." Catalogue from a traveling exhibit of the Connecticut Historical Society, 1984.

Corkin, Frank R., Jr. "The History of Middlesex Memorial Hospital, 1904-1971," paper, Middlesex Memorial Hospital, 1971.

Coyle, Barbara Carrington A. "An Investigation of Marriage Patterns of Middletown, Connecticut's Four Principal White Ethnic Groups, The Italians, Polish, Irish and Jews in Terms of Ethnicity and Religion, 1900-1979." In *Ethnic Heritage Studies Journal 1980.* Middletown, Connecticut: Graduate Liberal Studies Program, Wesleyan University, 1980.

Cunningham, Janice P. "National Register of Historic Places Nomination for North End Historic District, Middletown." Hartford, Connecticut: Connecticut Historical Commission, 1985.

Cunningham, Janice P. and Elizabeth A. Warner. *Portrait of A River Town: The History and Architecture of Haddam, Connecticut.* Middletown, Connecticut: The Greater Middletown Preservation Trust, 1984.

Daniels, Bruce C. *The Connecticut Town: Growth and Development, 1635-1790.* Middletown, Connecticut: Wesleyan University Press, 1979.

DeBoer, Gelle. Telephone interview with author, February 1990.

DeForest, John W. *History of the Indians of Connecticut from the Earliest known Period to 1850.* Hartford, Connecticut: Wm. Jas. Hamersley Publishers, 1851.

Delaney, Edmund, ed. and comp. *Life in the Connecticut River Valley 1800-1840, from the Recollections of John Howard Redfield.* Essex, Connecticut: Connecticut River Museum, 1988.

Delaney, Edmund. *The Connecticut River: New England's Historic Waterway.* Chester, Connecticut: The Globe Pequot Press, 1983.

Donlan, H. F. *The Middletown Tribune Souvenir Edition: An Illustrated and Descriptive Expositon of Middletown, Portland, Cromwell, East Berlin, and Higganum.* Middletown, Connecticut: E. F. Bigelow, 1896.

DuFour, Jeanne Louise. "Quality of Life and Transportation: A Study of Middletown." B. A. thesis, Wesleyan University, 1971.

Field, David Dudley. *A Statistical Account of Middlesex.* Middletown, Connecticut: Clark and Lyman, 1819.

Field, David D. *Centennial Address and Historical Sketches.* Middletown, Connecticut: William B. Casey, 1853.

Frayne, Thomas. Telephone interview with author, February 1990.

Gould, Sally Innis. "The Jews: Their Origins, In America, In Connecticut." *The Peoples of Connecticut Multicultural Ethnic Heritage Series.* Number three. Storrs, Connecticut: World Education Project, School of Education, University of Connecticut, 1980.

Greater Middletown Preservation Trust. *Middletown, Connecticut: Historical and Architectural Resources.* 3 vols. Middletown, Connecticut: The Greater Middletown Preservation Trust, 1979.

Gross, Robert A. *The Minutemen and their World.* New York: Hill and Wang, American Century Series, 1976.

Hall, Peter Dobkin. "Middletown: Streets, Commerce, and People, 1650-1981." *Wesleyan University Sesquicentennial Papers,* No. 8, 1981.

Hallock, Frank K. and James L. McConoughy. "A Pamphlet Containing Two Articles on Middletown and The Connecticut River," Middletown, Connecticut: General Tercentenary Committee, 1950.

Halloran, Frances W. and Betty Turco, comps. "Middletown, Connecticut Vignettes, In Celebration of the Nation's Bicentennial." Prepared for The City of Middletown Commission on the Arts and Cultural Activities, 1976.

Hamlin, Talbot. *Greek Revival Architecture in America.* London: Oxford University Press, 1944.

Harrington, Karl Pomeroy. *The Background of Wesleyan: A Study of Local Conditions about the Time the College was Founded.* Middletown, Connecticut: Wesleyan University, 1942.

Held, Lucas. "Plant Forged Key Role in World War II." *The Middletown Press.* February 3, 1989.

Janick, Herbert F., Jr. *A Diverse People: Connecticut, 1914 to the Present.* Chester: Pequot Press, 1975.

Janoch, Jeanne (Bladek), "The Greatest Changes in Middletown Since 1900." High School paper, Middletown High School, 1973.

Johnson, Reverend Alvin D. "A Brief History of the Connecticut State Hospital at Middletown, Connecticut." Middletown, Connecticut, undated (ca. 1955).

Johnson, Curtiss S. *Raymond E. Baldwin, Connecticut Statesman,* Chester, Connecticut: Pequot Press, 1972.

Knapp, Alfred P. *Connecticut Yesteryears: So Saith the Wind.* Old Saybrook, Connecticut: Alfred P. Knapp, 1985.

Lewis, Thomas R. and John E. Harmon. *Connecticut: A Geography.* Boulder, Colorado: Westview Press, 1986.

Lieberman, Meg. "Center Street in Transition: 1812-1868." Undergraduate paper, Wesleyan University, 1979.

Liss, Julia. "College Street: What Was There?" Undergraduate paper, Wesleyan University, 1978.

Lombardo, Joseph G. "Green Street: The Americanization of a Sicilian Village." Master's thesis, Wesleyan University, 1989.

McCallum, John D. *The Encyclopedia of World Boxing Champions.* Radnor, Pennsylvania: Chilton Book Company, 1975.

McKenna, Edward J. "The One Hundredth Anniversary of the Founding of Saint John's Parish, 1843-1943." Middletown, Connecticut, 1943.

Mercantile Publishing Company. "Leading Business Men of Middletown." Boston: Mercantile Publishing Company, 1890.

Meyers, John L. "Anti-Slavery Agents in Connecticut, 1833-1838." *Connecticut History Magazine,* a publication of The Association for the Study of State and Local History. (March 1983) no. 24.

Middlebrook, Louis F. *Maritime Connecticut During the Revolution.* 2 vols. Salem, Massachusetts: The Essex Institute, 1925.

Middlesex Mutual Assurance Company. *Centennial 1836-1936: A brief account of the more significant events in the history of the County of Middlesex and the growth of the Middlesex Mutual Assurance Company.* Middletown, Connecticut: Middlesex Mutual Assurance Company, 1936.

Middletown Press. "The Centennial Edition of the *Middletown Press, 1884-1984.*" Middletown, Connecticut: 1984.

Middletown Planning and Zoning Department. United State Census, Extracts from 1960, 1970, and 1980.

Middletown and Portland Directories. New Haven, Connecticut: Price and Lee Co., 1879 to 1945.

Middletown-Portland Bridge Committee. "The Middletown-Portland Bridge," Middletown, Connecticut: Middletown-Portland Bridge Committee, 1938.

Milano, Marche. "The Famine Generation: The Middletown Irish in the 1850s." Seminar paper, Wesleyan University, 1980.

Montgomery, Charles F. *A History of American Pewter.* New York: Praeger Publishers, 1973.

Nelligan, Tom. *The Valley Railroad Story: The Connecticut Valley Line.* New York: Quadrant Press, Inc., 1983.

O'Connor, David E. and Arthur E. Soderlind. "The Swedes: In their Homeland, In America, In Connecticut." *The Peoples of Connecticut Multicultural Ethnic Heritage Series.* Number 7. Storrs, Connecticut: The I. N. Thut World Education Center, The University of Connecticut, 1983.

Ohno, Kate. "National Register of Historic Places Nomination for the Connecticut General Hospital for the Insane." Hartford, Connecticut: Connecticut Historical Commission, 1983.

Parish, W. H. ed., *Scenes of Middlesex County.* Chicago: The W. H. Parish Publishing Company, 1892.

Penny Press. "Penny Press, Special Illustrated Edition." Middletown, Connecticut: The Penny Press, 1898.

Portland, Conn. Freestone Quarries, from *National Magazine,* Vol. 3 (1853), pp. 265-272, 361-367.

Potter, Lucy G. and William A. Ritchie. *The History and Architecture of East Hampton.* Middletown, Connecticut: The Greater Middletown Preservation Trust, 1980.

Price, Carl F. *Wesleyan's First Century.* Middletown: Wesleyan University, 1932.

Purcell, Richard J. *Connecticut in Transition, 1775-1818.* Middletown, Connecticut: Wesleyan University Press, 1963.

Redevelopment Agency for the City of Middletown. "Preliminary Redevelopment Plan for the Center Street-Court Place Redevelopment Area." Middletown, Connecticut, 1954.

Reynolds, John E. "The Artisans of Henshaw Lane: An Evaluation of the Role of Middletown, Connecticut as a Center of the Early American Pewter Industry." Undergraduate paper, Yale University, 1980.

Richter, Alice Bridge. *History of the Church of the Holy Trinity, Middletown, Connecticut*. Middletown, Connecticut: Alice Bridge Richter, 1963.

Roberts, Frank and Mildred. Interview with author. December, 1989.

Rose, James M. and Barbara W. Brown, *Tapestry: A Living History of the Black Family in Southeastern, Connecticut*. New London, Connecticut: New London County Historical Society, 1979.

Roth, David M. *Connecticut, A History*. New York: W. W. Norton & Company, Inc., 1979.

Sangree, Walter H. "Mel Hyblaeum: A Study of the People of Middletown of Sicilian Extraction with Special Emphasis on the Changes in their Values Resulting from Assimilation into the Middletown Community." Master's thesis, Wesleyan University, 1952.

Schorr, Brian. "A Narrative History of Prohibition in Middletown, Conn." Undergraduate paper, Wesleyan University, 1976.

Snow, Wilbert. *Codline's Child: The Autobiography of Wilbert Snow*. Middletown, Connecticut: Wesleyan University Press, 1968.

Souvenir Program: Seventh Annual Minstrel sponsored by the Russell Fire Department." Middletown, Connecticut, January 25, 1923.

Souvenir Program of the First Annual Ball given by the Police Benefit Association of Middletown, Connecticut." Middletown, Connecticut, January 17, 1924.

St. Mary of Czestochowa Church. "Diamond Jubilee of St. Mary of Czestochowa Parish, 1979." Middletown, Connecticut: St. Mary of Czestochowa Church, 1979.

St. Sebastian Church. "Fifty-Second Anniversary of St. Sebastian's Feast." Middletown, Connecticut: St. Sebastian Church, 1973.

Stone, Frank Andrews, comp. "The Irish: In their Homeland, In America, In Connecticut." *The Peoples of Connecticut Multicultural Ethnic Heritage Studies Series*. Number One. Storrs, Connecticut: World Heritage Project, the University of Connecticut, 1975.

Strother, Horatio T. *The Underground Railroad in Connecticut*. Middletown, Connecticut: Wesleyan University Press, 1962.

Tarallo, Frank J. "Frank Tarallo." In *The Immigrants Speak: Italian Americans Tell Their Story*, edited by Salvatore J. La Gumina. New York: Center for Migration Studies, 1979.

Tedone, David, ed. *A History of Connecticut's Coast*. Hartford, Connecticut: Department of Environmental Protection, Coastal Management Program, 1972.

Thomas, John Carl. *Connecticut Pewter and Pewterers*. Hartford, Connecticut: Connecticut Printers, Inc., 1976.

Trumbell, James Hammond. *Indian Names in Connecticut*. Hartford, Connecticut: Case, Lockwood and Brainerd Company, 1881; Reprint. Hamden, Connecticut: an Archon Book, an imprint of The Shoe String Press, Inc., 1974.

Turner, Gregg M. and Melancthon W. Jacobus. *Connecticut Railroads . . . An Illustrated History*. Hartford, Connecticut: The Connecticut Historical Society, 1986.

Van Dusen, Albert E. "Middletown and the American Revolution." Middletown, Connecticut: Rockfall Corporation and the Middlesex County Historical Society, 1950.

Wadsworth Atheneum, "The Great River Show: Art & Society of the Connecticut Valley, 1635-1820." Hartford, Connecticut: Wadsworth Atheneum, catalogue in conjunction with The Great River Show, 22 September 1985-6 January 1986.

Waldman, Carl *Encyclopedia of Native American Tribes*. New York: Facts on File Publications, 1988.

Wallace, Willard M. "Middletown Tercentenary, 1650-1950." Middletown, Connecticut: Middletown Tercentenary Commission, 1950.

Walters, Ian S., "The Changing Geography of Middletown, 1950-1965," Master's dissertation, University of Edinburgh, 1965.

Whipple, Chandler. *The Indian in Connecticut*. Stockbridge: Massachusetts: The Berkshire Traveller Press, 1972.

Whittemore, Henry. "History of Middletown." In *History of Middlesex County, Connecticut*, edited by J. B. Beers. New York: J. B. Beers and Company, 1884.

Wilbur, C. Keith. *The New England Indians*. Chester, Connecticut: The Globe Pequot Press, 1978.

Wilcox, Milo. Interview with author. Middletown, Connecticut, Summer 1989.

Woltmann, Regina. "A Neighborhood Study: The North End." Graduate paper, Graduate Liberal Studies Program, Wesleyan University, 1981.

Works Progress Administration. "Sketch of Maromas." Old Records Project #2507. Middletown, Connecticut: Works Progress Administration, 1937.

MAPS

Bailey, O. H. *Middletown, Connecticut*. O. H. Bailey and Company, 1877.

Barnum, H. L. *Map of the City of Middletown*. Middletown, Connecticut: J. T. Porter, engraver, 1825.

Clark, Richard. *Map of the City of Middletown*. New Haven, Connecticut: Richard Clark, 1851.

Map of Middlesex County, Connecticut from Surveys Under the Direction of H. L. Walling. New York: H. and C. T. Smith and Company, 1859.

Railroads, 52, 54-57, 78, 82, 91, 129, 140, 181
Rapallo Avenue, 78, 80, 113
Redevelopment, 80, 88, 94, 162-165, 166, 167
Redevelopment Agency, 163-166
Remington-Rand Company, 149, 155, 183
Reynolds, John F. III, 164, 166
Ridge Road, 132, 139, 140-141
River trade, 20-22, 28, 29, 30, 52, 59
Riverview Cemetery, 21, 56, 78
Riverview Center, 88, 163, 164
Roberts family, 127, 128, 131, 132
Rockfall Woolen Company, 182
Roosevelt, President Theodore, 145
Route 9, 162, 164
Russell Library, 48
Russell Manufacturing Company, 21, 37, 38, 41, 51, 52, 59, 84, 89, 106, 111, 130, 132, 136, 149, 157, 159, 172
Russell, Samuel, 20-22, 30, 31, 37, 48, 84, 90, 148, 177
Russell, Thomas MacDonough, 84

S

Saint John's Evangelical Lutheran Church, 85, 111-112, 136
Saint John's Roman Catholic Church, 100, 119, 173
Saint Kazimierz Society, 107-108
Saint Mary of Czestochow Church, 108, 111
Saint Paul's Evangelical Lutheran Church, 111-112, 114
Saint Sebastian Roman Catholic Church, 118, 119
Sawmill Race Track, 127
Schools, 44, 55, 76, 100, 110, 126, 127, 128, 132, 134, 138, 139, 148, 150, 151, 161, 173
Scovill family, 137, 139
Sentinel and Witness, 73
Shapiro family, 97, 98-99, 104, 106, 165
Shepard Block, 87
Shew, Dr. Abram, 46, 48, 49
Shipbuilding, 20, 42, 70, 178
Silver Manufacturing Company, 126, 129
Slavery, 59
Smith and Bishel Store, 95
Smith family, 125, 126, 128
Smith Grocery Store, M. A., 136, 184
Smith Manufacturing, J. O., 125, 126
South Congregational Church, 26, 28

South End, 90, 104-106, 164, 166, 173
South Farms, 61, 84, 85, 101, 111-112, 125, 130, 132, 136-139, 140-141, 184
South Green, 85, 164, 185, 186
South Main Street School, 151
South Street, 83, 103, 104
Southeast Asian immigration, 174
Sowheag, 19
Spanish-American War, 82
Standard Tire Company, 153, 159
Starr family, 33, 38, 178
Steamboat service, 52-55, 89, 146
Stiles and Parker Press Company, 67, 71, 80
Stow, Joshua, 33-35
Strict Congregational Society. See South Congregational Church
Stueck's Bakery, 51, 90, 91, 94, 111
Stueck's Modern Tavern, 90, 94, 95
Sumner Street, 83, 85, 103, 104, 173
Swedish Evangelical Lutheran Tabor Church, 112, 116
Swedish immigration, 112, 116-117

T

Third Congregational Church (Westfield), 126
Town Farm, 34
Town, Ithiel, 22, 30, 31
Trolley service, 54, 58, 78, 186
Truitt, Isaac, 62
Truman, President Harry S., 161
Tuttle Brick Company, 150, 170
Tynan, John, 161, 168

U

Underground Railroad, 60
Union Mills, 71, 72
Union Park. See South Green
Union Railroad Station, 78, 80, 91
Union Street, 71, 79, 104
United Technologies, 134
Universalist Church, 12

V

Victor Sewing Machine Company, 67
Vinal Technical School, 73
Vorwaerts Society, 113

W

Wadsworth, Colonel Clarence, 129, 135
Wadsworth Playground, 119
Wadsworth State Park, 129, 135

Wangunks, 18-19
War of 1812, 38
Warmsley family, 61, 62, 63, 81, 84
Washington Hotel, 43, 45
Washington Street, 90, 91, 146
Water Street, 79, 82
Watkinson family, 39, 60, 66, 69, 90
Watkinson Mill, 39, 66, 69
Webb, Isaac, 44-45, 79, 180
Wesleyan Hills Development, 129
Wesleyan University, 34, 38, 44-45, 60, 61, 62, 66-68, 74, 75, 84, 126, 129, 155, 168-170, 172, 174, 176, 181
Westfield, 106, 125-131, 192
Westfield Falls, 128, 143
Westfield Methodist Church, 1226
Westfield Railroad Station, 129
Westfield Residents for Rational Development, 127
Westfield Store, 130
Wetmore, Judge Seth, 25
Wiernasz, Joh, 103, 108, 110
Wilcox Lock Company, 10, 40
Wilcox, Crittenden and Company, 39, 52, 64-66, 69, 84, 106, 111, 132, 149, 157
Wilcox, Horace, 126, 127, 129
Wilcox, William Walter, 66, 147
Witness, 73
Women: in industry, 71; at Wesleyan, 75
Woodrow Wilson High School, 150, 170, 172
Woodward, Moses, 29, 32, 73
Woolworth, F. W., 51
Works Progress Administration (W.P.A.), 149, 152
World War I, 147
World War II, 120, 157-159

X

Xenelis family, 122-134

Y

Y.M.C.A., 92, 93, 96, 145
Young, James D., 97

Z

Zawisza family, 107-108

About the Author

❏

Elizabeth A. Warner was raised in Middletown, Connecticut, and attended public schools. She attended Grinnell College in Grinnell, Iowa, and received her bachelor of arts degree in history from the University of Connecticut.

Warner returned to Middletown after college and began working with the Greater Middletown Preservation Trust in 1980. She credits her early appreciation for local history to the strong sense of community and family heritage instilled by her parents and grandparents. With the Trust, Warner became involved in architectural resource surveys and public education programs. While working at the Trust, she co-authored *Portrait of a River Town: The History and Architecture of Haddam, Connecticut* in 1984 with Janice P. Cunningham, which was honored with 1985's Excellence in Community History Award by the American Association for State and Local History. Warner taught middle school history at the Independent Day School in Middlefield from 1985 to 1988. She anticipates returning to teaching, where she hopes to inspire a respect for history and an appreciation for the resources available within the community.